THE SHAKESPEARE PLAYS

MEASURE FOR MEASURE

THE SHAKESPEARE PLAYS

AS YOU LIKE IT
HENRY VIII
JULIUS CAESAR
MEASURE FOR MEASURE
RICHARD II
ROMEO AND JULIET

THE
SHAKESPEARE
PLAYS

Literary Consultant: John Wilders

Measure for Measure

MAYFLOWER BOOKS
NEW YORK

A BBC TV and Time-Life Television Coproduction.

Published in the United States by Mayflower Books Inc., New York City 10022.

Originally published in England by The British Broadcasting Corporation, 35 Marylebone High Street, London W1M 4AA, England.

The text of *Measure for Measure* used in this volume is the Alexander text, edited by the late Professor Peter Alexander and chosen by the BBC as the basis for its television production, and is reprinted by arrangement with William Collins Sons and Company Ltd. The complete Alexander text is published in one volume by William Collins Sons and Company Ltd under the title *The Alexander Text of the Complete Works of William Shakespeare*.

Library of Congress Cataloging in Publication Data

Shakespeare, William, 1564–1616.
  Measure for Measure.

  (His The BBC Shakespeare)
  I. Wilders, John. II. Title. III. Series: Shakespeare, William, 1564–1616. Selected works. 1978–
  PR2824.A23   1978   822.3'3   78–24112

ISBN 0–8317–5775–2

Manufactured in England

First American Edition

CONTENTS

PREFACE

Cedric Messina

Measure for Measure comes over with great force in this modern age, and for a play that has not been remarkable for the number of its revivals, those coming to it for the first time in this television production may well wonder why it has not been firmly established as a great favourite. Perhaps this production will help to redress the balance.

Justice for Justice might make an equally appropriate title for the play, for the whole work is permeated by the legal system of Vienna at the time of its writing. The plot, sensationally bloodied, can be traced back to a letter by a Hungarian student in 1547 in which is told the story of the judge and the girl who is persuaded to prostitute herself for her brother's life. *Measure for Measure* is described as a comedy, but it is only in the sub-plot, laid amongst the prostitutes and tapsters of the town, that laughs are to be found. The main plot revolves around the decision of the Duke of Vienna, Vincentio, to hand over the administration of justice to Angelo whilst he is to leave Vienna for Poland. The Duke feels that nineteen years of his permissive rule have been too long for him, a lenient man, to effect a necessary change. Angelo, acting as the judge, condemns a young man, Claudio, to death for immorality, for he has made a young girl of Vienna pregnant. His sister, Isabella, comes before Angelo to plead for his life, and so the scene is set for the two great confrontations between them. They give the play its great strength. In them Shakespeare makes some of his most eloquent pleas for justice and mercy. As the two protagonists confront each other, neither prepared to give an inch to the demands of the other, we see to what great heights dramatic writing can rise.

Angelo and Isabella are roles that are much sought after. In the contemporary theatre John Gielgud made a tremendous impact as Angelo, for this guilt-ridden man of rectitude has many great moments in the play. In this production Tim Pigott-Smith plays Angelo, and Isabella is the much acclaimed leading player from

6

both the Royal Shakespeare Company and the National Theatre, Kate Nelligan. She had never played Isabella before, and she gives a most remarkable performance of the girl rigid with moral fervour. In the lower depths the comics, led by Pompey, are more than the usual Shakespearian 'low comics', and the gadfly Lucio is a creation of original and effective force.

The only authoritative text for *Measure for Measure* is that published in the First Folio of the plays, of 1623, for it was never published in Quarto form before this date. If is also an inaccurate and confusing text, making the experts agree that it was probably copied from the prompt copy used by Shakespeare's company. The production was recorded in the BBC Television Centre between 17 and 22 May 1978.

Shakespeare's plays were not only performed in theatres, for one of the earliest references to performances of plays by Shakespeare was made by William Keeting, a Naval Commander who kept a journal of a voyage to the East Indies in 1607. The entry for 5 September, off the coast of Sierra Leone, refers to a performance of *Hamlet*, and that of 30 September to a performance of *Richard II*, both being performed for Portuguese visitors aboard the East India Company's ship the *Dragon*. And so the plays started their triumphant progress of performances throughout the civilised world.

BBC Television is not inexperienced in the presentation of the plays of William Shakespeare, and indeed as early as 1937, on the first regular television service in the world, it presented a full-length version of *Julius Caesar*. Since that date, thirty of the plays have been presented, the more popular ones many times over. Some have been produced in encapsulated form like *An Age of Kings*, some done on location like *Hamlet* at Elsinore with Christopher Plummer as the Prince and Robert Shaw as Claudius, and *Twelfth Night* at Castle Howard in Yorkshire with Janet Suzman leading the cast as Viola. Studio productions have included *The Tragedy of King Lear*, and *The Merchant of Venice* with Maggie Smith as a memorable Portia. Many productions have been taken from the theatre and translated into television terms like the Royal Shakespeare Company's *The Wars of the Roses* and The National Theatre Zeffirelli production of *Much Ado About Nothing*.

In the discharging of its many duties as a Public Broadcasting Service the BBC has presented during the last ten years, at peak viewing time on BBC 1 on every fourth Sunday night, *Play of the*

7

Month, a series of classical productions ranging from all the major plays of Chekhov to a number of Shavian masterpieces. Aeschylus has been produced in the series, and so have many of the plays of William Shakespeare. So not only in the presentation of Shakespeare, but also in the translation to the screen of the great dramatic statements of all ages and countries has the BBC demonstrated that it is fully equipped to meet the enormous challenge of *The BBC Television Shakespeare*.

The autumn of 1975 gave birth to the idea of recording the complete canon of the thirty-seven plays of the national playwright. (Thirty-six of the plays were published in the First Folio of 1623, exactly half of which had never been published before. The thirty-seventh is *Pericles, Prince of Tyre*, first published in the Quarto of 1609.) The first memo on the subject of televising all the plays emanated from my office on 3 November 1975, and was addressed to Alasdair Milne, then Director of Programmes, and now Managing Director, Television. We were asking for his blessing on the project. His reply was immediate and enthusiastic, as was that of the present Director-General, Ian Trethowan. This warm response to the idea stimulated us in the Plays Department to explore the possibility of making the plan a reality – six plays per year for six years, with one odd man out. It has been called the greatest project the BBC has ever undertaken.

There followed a succession of meetings, conferences, discussions and logistical quotations from engineers, designers, costume designers, make-up artists, financial advisers, educational authorities, university dons and musicians. The Literary Consultant, Dr John Wilders, was appointed, as was David Lloyd-Jones as Music Adviser. Alan Shallcross was made responsible for the preparation of the texts. On the island of Ischia, off the coast of Italy, Sir William Walton composed the opening fanfare for the title music for the series. Visits were made to the United States of America to finalise coproduction deals, decisions were taken about the length of the presentations to average about two-and-a-half hours per play, and more seriously, the order of their transmission. This was a game played by many interested parties, some suggesting the plays be presented chronologically, which would have meant the series opening with the comparatively unknown *Henry VI Parts 1, 2 and 3*. The idea was hastily abandoned. A judicious mixture of comedy, tragedy and history seemed the best answer to the problem. It was decided that the English histories, from *Richard II* through all the *Henry IVs*, *V* and *VIs* to *Richard III*, would be presented in chronological order, so that some day in the not too distant future, the eight plays that form this sequence will be able to be seen in their historical order, a unique record of the chronicled history of that time. The plays that form the first sequence will be *Romeo and Juliet, Richard II, As You Like It, Julius Caesar, Measure for Measure* and *Henry VIII*.

The guiding principle behind *The BBC Television Shakespeare* is to make the plays, in permanent form, accessible to audiences throughout the world, and to bring to these many millions the sheer delight and excitement of seeing them in performance, in many cases for the first time. For students, these productions will offer a wonderful opportunity to study the plays performed by some of the greatest classical actors of our time. But it is a primary intention that the plays are offered as entertainment, to be made as vividly alive as it is possible for the production teams to make them. They are not intended to be museum-like examples of past productions. It is this new commitment, for six plays of Shakespeare per year for six years, that makes the project unique.

In the thirty-seven plays there are a thousand speaking parts, and they demand the most experienced of actors and the most excellent of directors to bring them to life. In the field of directors we are very fortunate, for many of the brilliant practitioners in this series of plays have had wide experience in the classics, both on television and in the theatre. The directors are responsible for the interpretations we shall see, but as the series progresses it will be fascinating to see how many of the actors take these magnificent parts and make them their own.

It was decided to publish the plays, using the Peter Alexander edition, the same text as used in the production of the plays, and one very widely used in the academic world. But these texts with their theatrical divisions into scenes and acts are supplemented with their television equivalents. In other words we are also publishing the television scripts on which the production was based. There are colour and black and white photographs of the production, a general introduction to the play by Dr John Wilders and an article by Henry Fenwick which includes interviews with the actors, directors, designers and costume designers, giving their reactions to the special problems their contributions encountered in the transfer of the plays to the screen. The volumes include a newly compiled glossary and a complete cast list of the performers, including the names of the technicians, costume designers and scenic designers responsible for the play.

9

INTRODUCTION TO
MEASURE FOR MEASURE

John Wilders

Measure for Measure is one of the few plays of Shakespeare to which we can give a more-or-less precise date. In the account books of the Master of the Revels, the official responsible for providing entertainments for the monarch, there is an entry noting that a play called 'Mesur for Mesur' by 'Shaxberd' was performed in the banqueting hall of Whitehall on the night after Christmas 1604, presumably as part of the seasonal festivities and in the King's own presence.

If we compare *Measure for Measure* with any of Shakespeare's previous comedies we can see at once that he was here experimenting in a new kind of drama. In all his earlier comedies he had written chiefly about love, courtship and marriage. In *Measure for Measure*, however, he writes about sex and fornication. The settings for the earlier comedies had often been domestic: the houses of Baptista and Petruchio in *The Taming of the Shrew*, Leonato's estate in *Much Ado About Nothing* with his immediate family and guests, the households of Orsino and Olivia in *Twelfth Night* with their servants, Cesario and Malvolio. *Measure for Measure*, on the other hand, is very much a city comedy. It takes place in Vienna and, as the action moves from the ducal palace to the brothels, the convent, the courtroom and the prison, it portrays the richly-textured experiences of city life. It also conveys, like the greatest chronicles of the city, the novels of Dickens, the fragmentation of urban society. Just as in *Bleak House* the aristocracy exist in remote isolation from the crumbling, diseased tenements frequented by Jo the crossing sweeper, so in the opening scenes of this play the withdrawn, contemplative Duke, the fastidious scholar Angelo, and the ardent young novice Isabella lead separate lives, unaware of Pompey, Froth and Mistress Overdone whose haunts are the back streets and the brothels. And the high-principled solitaries discover, as they do in *Bleak House*, that their lives are linked with the criminal world in ways they had never supposed.

Measure for Measure was also, in its time, a fashionable play. Unlike Shakespeare's previous comedies it deals not so much with the problems of love and with domestic, household affairs, but with the problems of the community as a whole, with 'government', one of the very first words to be spoken in the dialogue. Its concern is specifically with the difficulties encountered by the ruler in his attempts to administer the law. This was the subject of a book which had been widely discussed during the year before the play was written, the *Basilicon Doron* (or 'Royal Gift'), the author of which was obviously the most prominent and noticeable member of the audience at that Christmastide production in 1604, James I himself. In his treatise on government, the King, who had come to the throne of England only a year previously, had observed that

> Lawes are ordained as rules of vertuous and sociall living, and not to be snares to trap your good subjects: and therefore the lawe must be interpreted according to the meaning, and not to the literall sense.

These reflections are, as we shall see, particularly relevant to the crises which develop during the play. Moreover, the presence of the new monarch, who was also the author of a book of instruction in government, gave a topical significance to the Duke's opening speech:

> Of government the properties to unfold
> Would seem in me t' affect speech and discourse,
> Since I am put to know that your own science
> Exceeds, in that, the lists of all advice
> My strength can give you.

This is not simply a compliment addressed by Duke Vincentio to his faithful counsellor but, at the same time, a courteous tribute by Shakespeare to his King, the patron of his theatrical company.

Measure for Measure was also a topical play, it has been suggested, in the choice of Angelo as its central character. His character was probably based on that of the strict puritans whose presence in English religious and social life was by then familiar. We may, today, assume that Shakespeare's introduction into the play of a law which defines adultery not simply as a sin but as a crime punishable by death was no more than a dramatic convention, highly improbable but necessary for the plot. In the early seventeenth century, however, it was far from improbable: the stricter puritans hoped to place such a law in the statute books if ever they came to political power.

It is with the problem of putting this law into effect that the action of *Measure for Measure* begins. Angelo, the newly-appointed deputy for the Duke, is determined to revive this neglected statute and to enforce it absolutely, but finds himself, immediately he takes office, confronted with what we should now call a test case, the case of Claudio. Claudio is practically the only major character in the play who is an ordinary, average man. The rest are, in one way or another, extremists. The characters are divided, roughly, between the whoremongers – Lucio, Pompey and Mistress Overdone – and the celibates – Angelo, Isabella and the Duke. Claudio, however, belongs to neither side. He is guilty, certainly, of adultery and is an acquaintance of Lucio's, but he also loves Juliet and is betrothed to her. By committing adultery with her before his actual marriage he is guilty, technically, of a capital offence, yet one which any young man might commit. As the Provost remarks,

> All sects, all ages, smack of this vice; and he
> To die for it!

In a play characterised by its intractable moral dilemmas, the problem of applying the law fairly in the case of Claudio is the first dilemma.

Towards Claudio's offence, the various characters express widely differing, indeed opposing attitudes, all of them simple and extreme. Lucio, apparently Mistress Overdone's most regular client, sees it as trivial and regards Angelo's severity as absurd:

> A little more lenity to lechery would do no harm in him . . .
> Why, what a ruthless thing is this in him, for the rebellion of a
> codpiece to take away the life of a man!

This is, of course, precisely the opinion we should expect from someone who spends his time in whorehouses and, moreover, Lucio has a special interest in the case of Claudio because, if the latter is executed, his own head will be at risk. Moreover, lenity towards lechery has been the policy adopted by the Duke with disastrous consequences: the city has degenerated into anarchic license, Vienna has spawned brothels like mushrooms, and the topic of conversation in them, as we soon discover, is not the pleasures of fornication but its after-effect, syphilis, an infection much less easily cured in Shakespeare's time than in our own, and therefore more terrifying. To overlook Claudio's crime of adultery is, therefore, not a satisfactory solution and, indeed, the Duke's failure to enforce the laws, and its unhappy consequences, is one reason for his retirement in favour of the rigorous Angelo.

The Deputy's attitude towards Claudio's offence is precisely the opposite of Lucio's, though equally simple, extreme and, again, characteristic of the man who expresses it. His own moral restraint, his strict control over his sexual appetites, is a quality which all the characters recognise. To the Duke, for example, Angelo is 'a man of stricture and firm abstinence', one who 'scarce confesses that his blood flows, or that his appetite is more to bread than stone'. As a man of absolute continency himself, Angelo has no hesitation in condemning Claudio to the block. Yet his point of view is no more satisfactory than Lucio's. Not only are there, in Claudio's case, extenuating circumstances, but the imposition of the law against adultery will have effects on his subjects of which Angelo is unaware. The demolition of the brothels will, from what we see of the city, cause widespread unemployment in Vienna, and professional bawds such as Pompey and his mistress will lose their livelihood. Moreover, as the more realistic characters frequently point out, adultery is so general a vice that, as Lucio observes,

> it is impossible to extirp it quite . . . till eating and drinking be put down.

The function of the law in any society is to protect its members against their own destructive or self-destructive appetites, whether for sexual satisfaction or for such obviously criminal activities as robbery or murder. This truth is grasped by the unfortunate criminal himself, Claudio, who does not deny his guilt nor is unwilling, at first, to endure the penalty:

> Our natures do pursue,
> Like rats that ravin down their proper bane,
> A thirsty evil; and when we drink we die.

Although laws are, therefore, necessary for the survival of a society, there appears to be no wholly acceptable way of applying them. Since the two conflicting attitudes towards Claudio's predicament are expressed with great conviction by the characters, the audience is itself forced into a dilemma, made more acute by their recognition that the man on trial is their own representative, the average man.

These two extreme positions, the one of lenience, the other of rigidity, are brought into direct conflict in the two most intensely dramatic scenes in the play, the interviews between Isabella and Angelo (II ii and II iv), which in turn give rise to a moral dilemma of a different kind. The basis of Isabella's plea to Angelo for mercy towards her brother is, yet again, consistent with what we know of her. As a young woman devoutly committed to the religious life, she invokes Christ's injunction 'Let him that is among you without sin cast the first stone', or, in her own words to Angelo,

> Go to your bosom,
> Knock there, and ask your heart what it doth know
> That's like my brother's fault. If it confess
> A natural guiltiness such as is his,
> Let it not sound a thought upon your tongue
> Against my brother's life.

No doubt we sympathise with her argument more strongly than with any other we have so far heard, yet Angelo's defence is also persuasive:

> It is the law, not I condemn your brother.
> Were he my kinsman, brother, or my son,
> It should be thus with him.

In other words, the law embodies principles which exist irrespective of the judge whose duty it is to safeguard them. Yet, although our sympathies may be divided between Isabella, who is after all trying desperately to save the life of her own brother, and Angelo who, however uncongenial personally, adheres to an irrefutable principle, neither is allowed to convince the other. For Isabella has, unknowingly, been testing Angelo at his weakest point: in the process of pleading for clemency towards Claudio's crime of adultery she has aroused the sexual appetite of Angelo himself. The underlying impulse behind Angelo's castigation of vice has been an unconscious sense of similar inclinations within himself. He has been punishing others for the weakness which he has himself with shame and difficulty repressed.

The first of these two great scenes is therefore the testing of Angelo. The second is the testing of Isabella, who is forced to make a choice between satisfying Angelo's lust as the price for her brother's reprieve, and rejecting his advances and thereby voluntarily allowing Claudio to be executed. In short, she must choose between the sacrifice of her virginity and the sacrifice of her brother. In the first of the two scenes Isabella unwittingly tests Angelo's sexual restraint; in the second Angelo tests Isabella's sense of compassion, ironically the very quality she had formerly tried to awaken in Angelo. But whereas the result of their first encounter is to break down Angelo's defences, the result of the second is to force Isabella into a more extreme religious and moral rigidity:

> Then, Isabel, live chaste, and, brother, die:
> More than our brother is our chastity.

Shakespeare has now shifted our attention from the apparently insoluble problem of Claudio to the intolerable dilemma of Isabella. Whether or not we support her resolution to protect her chastity at the expense of Claudio's life will depend very much on our own character and attitudes: the audience is again placed in the position of judge, and different readers have pronounced very different verdicts. The eighteenth-century critic Charlotte Lennox denounced Isabella as 'a mere vixen in her virtue' with 'the manners of an affected prude'. The nineteenth-century critic Mrs Jameson, on the other hand, saw in her 'a certain moral grandeur, a saintly grace, something of a vestal dignity. . . . She is like a stately and graceful cedar, towering on some alpine cliff, unbowed and unscathed amid the storm'. Isabella's problem, like the case of Claudio, is one to which there is no wholly right solution.

Our attention is now transferred to the prison where Claudio is waiting to hear the result of his sister's intercession and, meanwhile, is being prepared by the Duke for death. Here, once more, we are shown two extreme and conflicting points of view, each consistent with the man who expresses it. In making the condemned man ready for execution, the Duke, in his disguise as a friar, argues that life is so inherently painful and corrupt that death should not be feared but welcomed as a release:

> Reason thus with life.
> If I do lose thee, I do lose a thing
> That none but fools would keep. A breath thou art,
> Servile to all the skyey influences,
> That dost this habitation where thou keep'st
> Hourly afflict.

For the moment, the Duke's words of comfort convince Claudio that death is preferable to life, but when his sister announces that she has rejected Angelo's offer, he instantly changes his attitude

from one of stoical resignation to terror and panic at the prospect
of his imminent dispatch into the unknown:

Ay, but to die, and go we know not where;
To lie in cold obstruction, and to rot;
This sensible warm motion to become
A kneaded clod; and the delighted spirit
To bathe in fiery floods or to reside
In thrilling region of thick-ribbed ice;
To be imprison'd in the viewless winds,
And blown with restless violence round about
The pendant world; or to be worse than worst
Of those that lawless and incertain thought
Imagine howling – 'tis too horrible.

Having been persuaded, a few moments earlier, that life was not
worth living, Claudio is now convinced that death is too terrifying
to contemplate. Like all the major characters, Claudio is first
wrenched from one extreme attitude to its opposite and, as a
result, finds himself in an insupportable dilemma. Neither death
nor life appear to him acceptable. There is, needless to say, no
other choice available to him.

The role of the Duke is the longest in the play and he dominates
the last two acts. It is, as any actor who has played the part will
confirm, a very difficult one to interpret with any psychological
consistency. He is first shown to have been a dangerously
indulgent ruler whose neglect of the law has allowed the city to
become corrupt, and then to have foisted his problems on a
substitute whose reliability is, as he himself suspects, uncertain.
Although, to himself, he defends his actions as necessary for the
moral education of Angelo, nevertheless the Deputy is tested at a
very high cost: Claudio is made to believe that his execution is
imminent and Isabella is allowed to think, almost until the end of
the play, that Claudio is dead. On the other hand the Duke
delivers a number of general observations on the nature of
government of which, apparently, Shakespeare intended us to
approve, and it is he who makes the most spectacular appearance
'like power divine' in order to dispense justice in the closing scene.
It may be, however, that Shakespeare intended *Measure for
Measure* to show the trial and education of the Duke as well as of
Angelo and Isabella, and that this provides some explanation for
the apparent inconsistencies in his character.

To begin with, the Duke appears self-assured and certain of his shrewdness in judging other people, his corresponding knowledge of himself, and his power to intervene and resolve any difficulties which may arise during his supposed absence. In all three respects he discovers he has been self-deceived. He assumes that Angelo, having spent the night with Mariana, will be a man of his word and pardon the condemned Claudio, whereas Angelo actually confirms the order for Claudio's execution. He prides himself as one who, in the words of Escalus, 'contended especially to know himself', yet discovers that his reputation, at least with Lucio, is quite different from what he had supposed: 'a very superficial, ignorant, unweighing fellow'. He imagines he can save Claudio from execution by placing Barnardine on the block instead, but discovers that Barnardine is not willing to co-operate. Deprived of his robes of office he is less able to manipulate and control than he had imagined. And when, as Duke, he reappears to pass formal judgement on the guilty, his attempts to resolve the problems he has created are not wholly satisfactory, for no such resolutions are possible.

When Angelo's guilt is finally exposed and he stands ashamed, repentant and begging for death, the Duke awards him life and marriage to the woman he has formerly rejected. The unfortunate Lucio is first condemned to death for slander but then allowed to live and compelled to marry a whore, a sentence which the accused regards as worse than death. To Isabella, the devout religious celibate, he proposes marriage, an invitation which, significantly, she greets with silence. Although *Measure for Measure* concludes, like the earlier comedies, with the prospect of several marriages, none of them seems likely to succeed. It is a comedy which seems designed to show the impossibility of writing comedy.

The underlying cause of the insoluble dilemmas which characterise this uniquely philosophical play is the essentially divided nature of man. Shakespeare recognises that we are individuals with demanding impulses and desires of our own, but that we are also members of a community with an obligation to control our own wills for the sake of peace, stability and the common good. Whereas the unrestrained pursuit of personal appetite leads to anarchy, the rigid application of the law leads to injustice. Moreover, the presence of Isabella reminds us that we also have an obligation to God and that this may conflict with our obligation to our fellow men. The unresolved conflicts in *Measure for Measure* arise because the human condition is itself one of conflict. The cumbersome, half-satisfactory resolution which the Duke supplies is perhaps, under the circumstances, no worse than we can expect.

THE PRODUCTION

Henry Fenwick

Measure for Measure has had an uneven critical career: too rough hewn a piece to be labelled and explained satisfactorily by the critics, too intellectual perhaps for thoroughly popular appeal, but too strong to be dismissed as a minor work, it has been continually taken up by new commentators, examined, interpreted and set aside again. It is an enigmatic and intriguing play. 'Of the lesser known plays,' says producer Cedric Messina, 'it seemed to me that *Measure for Measure* was one of the best. I think it emerges in production – not only this production but in the two or three productions I've seen – as an enormously powerful, extraordinarily modern piece. It gets under your skin.'

'Modern' sounds at first, as Messina acknowledges, an odd adjective for a play whose plot revolves around a man condemned to death for fornication and a novice nun's defence of her chastity against a corrupt judge. But it is certainly true that the play has a strong pull today; Isabella's impassioned purity, and her unbendable will, make her almost a feminist heroine, and the play's sour ambiguities of attitude appeal to our own uncertainty. 'People go on about the sexuality of the play,' says Messina; 'Angelo's attack on a novice has always been considered rather shocking. But the play's real power lies in the two great interviews between Angelo and Isabella. And I did feel that the play would be enhanced by television because of the smallness of the confrontations, the duologues between the characters. There's no need for scenic background, just terrific intensity between these two people. Television brings that out enormously.'

Tim Pigott-Smith (*The Glittering Prizes*, *Eustace and Hilda*) was cast as the corrupted Angelo, a part that was in recent years most blazingly interpreted by Sir John Gielgud; and Kate Nelligan (*La Dame aux Camellias*, *Licking Hitler*) was Isabella, a heroine whose icy virtue has infuriated many in the past. 'I cast the girl first,' says Messina. 'I really felt that she was the pivot on which the whole thing turned.' He had already been struck by Kate Nelligan's strength, coolness and beauty – particularly in the National Theatre's production of *Heartbreak House*. Director Desmond Davis had worked with Tim on *Eustace and Hilda* and been excited by his work and by his camera presence. 'He had been with the RSC (Royal Shakespeare Company) for several years and at the Bristol Old Vic and at the National, and he was ready for Angelo.'

As might be expected from his background, first as a film cameraman and later as director of such movies as *The Girl with Green Eyes* and *I Was Happy Here*, Desmond Davis brings a strikingly filmic approach and frame of reference to this, his first Shakespearian directorial assignment. 'I felt that the audience I was interested in was perhaps a very young audience, had probably seen no Shakespeare at all, perhaps didn't go to the theatre a lot. I certainly didn't want to do a very scholastic production in a very reverent way – though obviously there was to be fidelity to the text. I wanted to do a rather colloquial production, so I did a few things like – for example, the long sequence in the jail: I made it like an AIP horror movie jail, flambeaux and red lighting and dwarf jailers. You wouldn't have been surprised if Peter Lorre had walked through the background. And I tried to make Mistress Overdone's brothel a bit like the *Destry Rides Again* saloon. I had the men smoking cigars and young ladies parading along the balconies. I wanted to make it like a western, with gambling games – so it's recognisable to a modern audience. I didn't want to get too involved in utter historical accuracy: it's an imaginative Vienna, but then – so is Shakespeare's. I wanted to get the feeling of a very dark, sinful city where no light got in and so it was never day – it was always either sunrise or sunset or dawn or dusk, the streets have mist in them. If you analyse the production it only becomes daylight in Act V when the whole thing's resolved.'

Because of apparent corruptions or confusions in the text as it exists the play poses a lot of problems, and there was a great deal of basic text work to be done. Here director and script editor Alan Shallcross had to work together long and closely. 'Desmond and I went through every single solitary word of the text together,' says Shallcross, 'dividing the play into television scenes as he began to build up his images, and that process inevitably involved coming to decisions about the text. We cut very little. There were two main cutting processes: first the mechanical cuts, what I call the stage-management cuts – lines meant to get people on and off stage, which you don't need for television. Second, we tried to rationalise the end of the play. When the Duke returns he alerts

19

various courtiers – the bureaucrats who are going to stage-manage his re-entry into Vienna. New characters are introduced and never seen again. I *think* Shakespeare's intention was to "give dreadful note of preparation", a build-up to the last scene, seeing the wheels of bureaucracy move and the forces crowding in on Angelo. But if that's so, I don't think it works. We rationalised it by taking it all out, leaving just enough in to make sure that the story is clear. These were the two major areas of excision.'

But the script editor's most nightmarish task was trying to straighten out Shakespeare's confused time sequences. Shakespeare is not known for the technical perfection of his time-keeping in his plays: the dramatically distorted time-scale of *Othello* is perhaps his most notorious piece of theatrical sleight of hand. But *Measure for Measure* is just as muddled. 'There are major errors of timing. Shakespeare cared nothing at all for consistency in time – he was only worried about the dramatic effect at any one moment in the play and very often contradicted himself: if he wants to make a scene dark for atmospheric reasons he will; then in the next scene he'll have someone say, "Why is it so light?" In *Measure for Measure* it's a nightmare: the vital factor in timing is the execution of Claudio: Angelo consistently talks about when he's going to be put to death. Now the stay of execution is Isabella's primary intention: but if you go through the play very carefully you find that her visits to Angelo and Angelo's insistence on Claudio's death at a certain time actually contradict each other. It has been the subject of a large number of detailed works that can drive you raving mad. One of the things I always do in preparing a text for rehearsal is to go through it – with ice on my head – and work out a logic, if logic exists; to expose the inconsistencies where they exist, and document the evidence to enable us to make a decision about whether we should simply go along with Shakespeare and risk confusing people, or whether we'll alter lines or sequences of days so that they make sense. But after doing it for six plays you find it actually doesn't matter too much: Shakespeare is far too good a dramatist, or at any rate far too good a man of the theatre, far too good a showbiz character to have allowed a situation to exist that gets in the way of the appreciation of the drama. He would have stood there and said, "You're wasting your time – they'll never remember." He uses his time for dramatic purposes and breaks his own logic. And if he doesn't care about it there's a sense in which we don't have to care. But for practical reasons on television you need to know what time it is, the director has to indicate what time of day he's playing a scene. A whole lighting plot has to be built upon the decision whether it's day or night, you have got to have worked out a fairly detailed time scheme. Shakespeare doesn't do that, and you have nothing to go on but what the text says.'

Television also brought out other practical problems which a stage production can more easily gloss over: the problem of the language of the crowd scenes. Traditionally, stage crowds are said to murmur 'rhubarb, rhubarb' to each other to give the impression of crowd noise, though most actors are a little more creative than that. 'In *Measure for Measure* there are two major scenes where there are a lot of people talking,' Shallcross points out. 'The first one is the scene (I ii) in the brothel with Mistress Overdone, where Lucio and the various gentlemen are talking and there's a lot of brothel chat. It would be pointless having background lines like "Will you have another half?" or "What's yours?", so I actually had to write Elizabethan rhubarb and create characters who might be there to speak it. Also there's a moment when Ms Overdone is being arrested in the brothel where I had to write a lot of dialogue for whores who are being taken out of their rooms and carted off to prison. All that had to be in quasi-authentic cod Elizabethan language and syntax. That's very important. It's important on stage but it's much more important on television because of the greater intimacy and immediacy. While the director chooses what you will see and what you will hear, nevertheless in the process of that selection you are bound to be closer to what's going on in the middle ground than you are in the theatre. So that does become a real problem on television. As a matter of fact I think it's a real problem in the theatre and not always solved. You can drop your period truthfulness very fast if you're not careful.'

Although Desmond Davis says he is not in pursuit of total historical accuracy, all the television Shakespeares have been anxious to maintain period truthfulness. This has often put an unusual strain on the costume department, since stage productions of Shakespeare have not made such stringent demands and therefore costumes already in existence that might be hired for the extras are not large in number. For *Measure for Measure* Odette Barrow needed costumes of the time of the first presentation of the play – the first years of the reign of James I. However, the English dress of that exact period was stiff and hard to work with for actors – ruffs and farthingales are limiting accessories. 'I went to the German Institute to see if there was anything I could use as a model, but there were so few artists working between 1599 and

1630 that it was terribly difficult. I found one artist I based a lot on – an Italian who worked most of the time in Holland and France.' In fact, the final costumes owed a good deal to Italian models. 'In that period the Italian style was less elaborate: they have always gone in for the softer style of costume. And it's quite possible that in Vienna there would have been some Italian influence.'

The character of the Duke of *Measure for Measure*'s Vienna has been the subject for much critical exploration and argument. No point here in rehearsing the various analyses of this figure who, in human terms, is, as Messina comments, 'inexplicable'. 'The Duke is a very, very misty sort of character,' says Davis. 'He was based loosely on James I. Shakespeare wrote this in 1604. When it was first presented Elizabeth had just died, James had come to the throne. James was very much like the Duke: he'd written many discourses on law himself, he hated crowds – he wouldn't go out among the crowds. When he did go out it was thought he sometimes went out in disguise. I got the picture of this man from looking at pictures of James.

'The Duke's motives are very strange; he acts almost irrationally at times throughout the play. He's Mr Fixit, moving from place to place behind the scenes, organising, withholding the truth from people. In my more irreverent moments I deem God to be like that: you see God doing such strange things around the world. In a playful way the Duke was rather like God, testing us, telling you with a bland face that you're on the right road when just at that moment the banana skin is in front of you. Ken [Colley, playing the Duke] is a remarkably clever and shrewd actor and I wanted to develop these qualities. I hope at times there's a light humour brought in. I didn't want a solid classical figure going through the action – I wanted a recognisable human being who nevertheless has some godlike properties. I also thought it essential that the Duke is seen to be weaker than Angelo, otherwise, the plot doesn't work, in my opinion.

'The play opens with the Duke summoning Angelo, and I brought Angelo in on a very big sweep. I'd kept off tracking shots before that because I rather wanted the Duke muted: I feel as a man he didn't use power – otherwise Vienna presumably wouldn't be in such a mess, with the law not being applied. I felt he was a bit of a dilettante – he preferred his science, he hated meeting people, he just left it all to Escalus. One felt he was very intelligent and very well meaning and very humane, but wasn't really a man of action. So I kept him rather still in those opening sequences. Then when he said, "Bid come before us Angelo", I brought Tim in on a jump cut and swept him down the entire length of the room, to give a feeling that *now* in comes Mr Powerful.'

Isabella and Angelo were clearer characters, though the character of Isabella, like the play itself, has gone through vicissitudes of critical approval and disapproval. At times praised for her chastity, at other times the character's virtue has been seen as reprehensible – even neurotic. Kate Nelligan is quite clear-minded about her: 'I had one and only one idea – opinion rather – from the day I first read it, which was the day I was offered it. I held the same view from the beginning to the end and I hold it now very strongly: the school of thought that considers Isabella a sexual neurotic and the play a treatise on repressive sexuality is absolute nonsense to me. It seems a much bigger play than that. He's not really interested in the sexual psychology of one woman and he certainly doesn't write plays about it. There's a completely forceful text argument that she's an incredibly strong-minded, eloquent, genuine, feeling, warm good woman who's caught in an intolerable position. Because religion has become a somewhat discredited pastime the modern view is that anyone who believes in heaven and hell as physical realities must be crazy. It seems to me perfectly acceptable that moral good and evil are forces which people will lay down their lives for. She is willing to; she says,

> Were it but my life
> I'd throw it down for your deliverance
> As frankly as a pin

and she means it. But her eternal life and her brother's eternal life are more important to her. I don't see that that springs from an unnatural repugnance to sexuality. It comes from a convinced passion – a passionate belief.'

There were at times difficulties balancing the Angelo/Isabella scenes, but as Davis explained: 'Both Tim and Kate are extremely fine actors and they loved their parts: they knew, as actors do, they sensed that the centre of the play is their antagonism. Shakespeare really wrote between Angelo and Isabella a sort of mirror image of two people: they have a lot of the same qualities – both rather emphatic in their judgements, both without tremendous breadth of imagination, both of them wanting to be right and good. There's a very natural clash between them, and as actors Tim and Kate bring it off wonderfully. The very first time we rehearsed the scene of their first meeting and confrontation you could feel the rehearsal room quiet down, all sorts of exciting undercurrents were going on. But it took us a long time to get the balance right between them. It was just shot very simply: two cameras the whole time, two opposed cameras that did the whole thing – a very simple piece of shooting that looked rather complex. It was a visual idea: he was rather large, shot from waist level, and she was a minute figure, shot using the whole depth of the room. Then slowly they come together. You always have this horror that you'll get it dead right in rehearsal, then something will go wrong when you record, some nuance will be missing. But God was with us in the studios.'

The scene of the confrontation is indeed strikingly set, acted and shot, subtle use being made of the enormous judgement hall and the impressively bureaucratic furnishings designer Stuart Walker has provided. 'People who are interested in power – and Angelo was obviously very interested in power, really loved it – would have a huge desk and secretaries and be signing and stamping things: he'd administrate beautifully – without much imagination or emotion but he'd be very efficient – and I thought a person like that, with a lot of weaknesses deep in his psyche, would hide behind this barricade of efficiency. He needs not to use his imagination, refuses to face his emotions. He hides behind the mechanics of power, work and administration. Every whizz kid who has to overwork is either running from despair or from some emotion he can't face: Angelo is doing this. I tried to set the scene so it would reflect these qualities. It is the first time we see him after he's taken over power, and I thought he'd set himself up so that anybody who came to see him would meet this enormous desk and would be cramped in a little end of the room, while he has the entire length of the room behind him, culminating in the throne and the crest and shield.'

More than most directors, says Stuart Walker, Davis works extremely closely with the set designer; strong visual images are in his mind from the outset and consequently he has clear ideas of how the set should look. At the outset of the play the action moves rapidly from palace to prison, brothel to convent, and the relation between the sets is striking. 'The brothel and the convent were the same set,' Davis points out. 'We simply repainted it white, took out the whores and the gaming tables and put in a statue of the Virgin Mary; changed the young ladies parading the upper level and put in some novices. The little doors and cells, instead of being used for whoring, are used for praying. Eroticism is the other side of purity – they are mirror images in man's psyche: a sad and unfortunate truth. We shot all the brothel scenes, then repainted the set in one day and shot the convent scene in the evening.'

Such swift economies were common. The sets, often enormous, doubled up and were consumed into each other, making huge demands on the ingenuity of the designer. Parts of the jail, stripped of bars, became distant street scenes; the nunnery, recycled, became part of the city gates – all in the interests not only of economy but also of greater vistas and effects of space. 'If you keep moving you subliminally feel there's a lot of space,' says Davis. 'The arrest of Claudio and the arrest of Pompey were done in long tracking shots: I hope it looked as though we were going down endless streets, but what we were really doing was going round and round the studio. Poor Stuart had to provide set all the way round. The camera actually went eight times round the stage in a continuous track, which meant feeding all that supply cable to it so that it had to be wrapped round the studio eight times.

'If it looks filmic I think the secret is in using space more, not being frightened of the multi-camera system. Have the confidence that the cameras and sound men will cope – as they will: curse you they may, but they cope. Any idiot can do close-ups against three feet of flock wallpaper, but if you have a great set it's really stupid not to use it, use the whole depth. I think there's a slight tendency in television to work too much in close-up and you get head upon head upon head. While it's very clear it doesn't express the poetry of movement, and I find after a while I lose the geography of a scene – I've forgotten how big the figures are or how far apart they are. I think you've got to choreograph your shooting and think very carefully before you get into huge heads.'

Only for the end of the play, under Davis's direction, is there a sense of the theatrical rather than the filmic and this was conscious choice. The end has been criticised for being too mechanical, too schematic, but Davis saw a shape there: 'Looking at Act V I felt the whole resolution was like a play within a play. Taking the hint from that, I provided the bare bones of an Elizabethan theatre: a rostrum backed with a throne. The courtiers and the people of Vienna became an audience. I felt the Duke was staging a show for them to demonstrate the meaning of the play. Shakespeare is trying to show us that what works for man is justice tempered with mercy, and Act V becomes a demonstration of that through the Duke. There's a theatricality about it. The light has been let in and the Duke brings the final message of the play: Justice, Grace and Mercy, I suppose.'

THE BBC TV CAST AND
PRODUCTIVE TEAM

The cast for the BBC television production was as follows:

THE DUKE	Kenneth Colley
ISABELLA	Kate Nelligan
ANGELO	Tim Pigott-Smith
CLAUDIO	Christopher Strauli
LUCIO	John McEnery
MARIANA	Jacqueline Pearce
POMPEY	Frank Middlemass
PROVOST	Alun Armstrong
MISTRESS OVERDONE	Adrienne Corri
ELBOW	Ellis Jones
FROTH	John Clegg
BARNARDINE	William Sleigh
ABHORSON	Neil McCarthy
JULIET	Yolande Palfrey
FRANCISCA	Eileen Page
ESCALUS	Kevin Stoney
FRIAR THOMAS	Godfrey Jackman
FIRST GENTLEMAN	Alan Tucker
SECOND GENTLEMAN	John Abbott
A JUSTICE	David Browning
SERVANT	Geoffrey Cousins
PAGEBOYS	David King Lassman
	Tony Friel
	Harry Jones
	John Sarbutt
	Nicholas Tudor
PRODUCTION ASSISTANT	Diarmuid Lawrence
PRODUCTION UNIT MANAGER	Fraser Lowden
MUSIC	James Tyler and the
	London Early Music Group

MUSIC ADVISER	David Lloyd-Jones
LITERARY CONSULTANT	John Wilders
MAKE-UP ARTIST	Cecile Hay-Arthur
COSTUME DESIGNER	Odette Barrow
SOUND	Chick Anthony
LIGHTING	Sam Barclay
DESIGNER	Stuart Walker
SCRIPT EDITOR	Alan Shallcross
PRODUCER	Cedric Messina
DIRECTOR	Desmond Davis

The production was recorded between 17 and 22 May 1978

THE TEXT

In order to help readers who might wish to use this text to follow the play on the screen the scene divisions and locations used in the television production and any cuts and rearrangements made are shown in the right-hand margins. The principles governing these annotations are as follows:

1. Where a new location (change of set) is used by the TV production this is shown as a new scene. The scenes are numbered consecutively, and each one is identified as exterior or interior, located by a brief description of the set or the location, and placed in its 'time' setting (e.g. Day, Night, Dawn). These procedures are those used in BBC Television camera scripts.

2. Where the original stage direction shows the entry of a character at the beginning of a scene, this has not been deleted (unless it causes confusion). This is in order to demonstrate which characters are in the scene, since in most cases the TV scene begins with the characters 'discovered' on the set.

3. Where the start of a TV scene does not coincide with the start of a scene in the printed text, the characters in that scene have been listed, *unless* the start of the scene coincides with a stage direction which indicates the entrance of all those characters.

4. Where the text has been cut in the TV production, the cuts are marked by vertical rules and by a note in the margin. If complete lines are cut, these are shown as, e.g., Lines 27–38 omitted. If part of a line only is cut, or in cases of doubt (e.g. in prose passages), the first and last words of the cut are also given.

5. Occasionally, and only when it is thought necessary for comprehension of the action, a note of a character's moves has been inserted in the margin.

6. Where composite sets are used or where the action moves from one part of a set to another, no attempt has been made to show this as a succession of scenes.

ALAN SHALLCROSS

28

MEASURE FOR MEASURE

DRAMATIS PERSONÆ

VINCENTIO, *the Duke.*
ANGELO, *the Deputy.*
ESCALUS, *an ancient Lord.*
CLAUDIO, *a young gentleman.*
LUCIO, *a fantastic.*
Two other like gentlemen.
VARRIUS, *a gentleman, servant to the Duke.*
PROVOST.
THOMAS, ⎫ *two friars.*
PETER, ⎭
A JUSTICE.
ELBOW, *a simple constable.*
FROTH, *a foolish gentleman.*

POMPEY, *a clown and servant to Mistress Overdone.*
ABHORSON, *an executioner.*
BARNARDINE, *a dissolute prisoner.*

ISABELLA, *sister to Claudio.*
MARIANA, *betrothed to Angelo.*
JULIET, *beloved of Claudio.*
FRANCISCA, *a nun.*
MISTRESS OVERDONE, *a bawd.*

LORDS, OFFICERS, CITIZENS, BOY, *and* ATTENDANTS.

THE SCENE : *Vienna.*

In the television production the part of VARRIUS has been omitted and the characters of Friar Thomas and Friar Peter are amalgamated into one as FRIAR THOMAS

ACT ONE.

SCENE I. *The Duke's palace.*

Enter DUKE, ESCALUS, LORDS, *and* ATTENDANTS.

DUKE. Escalus !
ESCAL. My lord.
DUKE. Of government the properties to unfold
    Would seem in me t' affect speech and discourse,
    Since I am put to know that your own science   5
    Exceeds, in that, the lists of all advice
    My strength can give you ; then no more remains
    But that to your sufficiency—as your worth is able—
    And let them work. The nature of our people,   10
    Our city's institutions, and the terms
    For common justice, y'are as pregnant in
    As art and practice hath enriched any
    That we remember. There is our commission,
    From which we would not have you warp. Call hither,   15
    I say, bid come before us, Angelo. [*exit an* ATTENDANT.
    What figure of us think you he will bear ?
    For you must know we have with special soul
    Elected him our absence to supply ;
    Lent him our terror, dress'd him with our love,   20
    And given his deputation all the organs
    Of our own power. What think you of it ?
ESCAL. If any in Vienna be of worth

SCENE I
Interior. The Duke's Audience Chamber. Sunset.

To undergo such ample grace and honour,
It is Lord Angelo.

Enter ANGELO.

DUKE. Look where he comes. 25 'Look where he comes'
ANG. Always obedient to your Grace's will, omitted.
 I come to know your pleasure.
DUKE. Angelo,
 There is a kind of character in thy life
 That to th' observer doth thy history
 Fully unfold. Thyself and thy belongings 30
 Are not thine own so proper as to waste
 Thyself upon thy virtues, they on thee.
 Heaven doth with us as we with torches do,
 Not light them for themselves ; for if our virtues
 Did not go forth of us, 'twere all alike 35
 As if we had them not. Spirits are not finely touch'd
 But to fine issues , nor Nature never lends
 The smallest scruple of her excellence
 But, like a thrifty goddess, she determines
 Herself the glory of a creditor, 40
 Both thanks and use. But I do bend my speech
 To one that can my part in him advertise.
 Hold, therefore, Angelo—
 In our remove be thou at full ourself ;
 Mortality and mercy in Vienna 45
 Live in thy tongue and heart. Old Escalus,
 Though first in question, is thy secondary.
 Take thy commission.
ANG. Now, good my lord,
 Let there be some more test made of my metal,
 Before so noble and so great a figure 50
 Be stamp'd upon it.
DUKE. No more evasion !
 We have with a leaven'd and prepared choice
 Proceeded to you ; therefore take your honours.
 Our haste from hence is of so quick condition
 That it prefers itself, and leaves unquestion'd 55
 Matters of needful value. We shall write to you,
 As time and our concernings shall importune,
 How it goes with us, and do look to know
 What doth befall you here. So, fare you well.
 To th' hopeful execution do I leave you 60
 Of your commissions.
ANG. Yet give leave, my lord,
 That we may bring you something on the way.
DUKE. My haste may not admit it ;
 Nor need you, on mine honour, have to do
 With any scruple : your scope is as mine own, 65
 So to enforce or qualify the laws
 As to your soul seems good. Give me your hand ;
 I'll privily away. I love the people,
 But do not like to stage me to their eyes ;
 Though it do well, I do not relish well 70

Their loud applause and Aves vehement ;
Nor do I think the man of safe discretion
That does affect it.   Once more, fare you well.
ANG. The heavens give safety to your purposes !
ESCAL. Lead forth and bring you back in happiness !   75
DUKE. I thank you. Fare you well.   [exit.
ESCAL. I shall desire you, sir, to give me leave
    To have free speech with you ; and it concerns me
    To look into the bottom of my place :
    A pow'r I have, but of what strength and nature   80
    I am not yet instructed.
ANG. 'Tis so with me.   Let us withdraw together,
    And we may soon our satisfaction have
    Touching that point.
ESCAL.   I'll wait upon your honour.   [exeunt.

SCENE II. A street.

Enter LUCIO and two other Gentlemen.

LUCIO. If the Duke, with the other dukes, come not to composition
    with the King of Hungary, why then all the dukes fall upon the
    King.
1 GENT. Heaven grant us its peace, but not the King of Hungary's !
2 GENT. Amen.
LUCIO. Thou conclud'st like the sanctimonious pirate that went to
    sea with the Ten Commandments, but scrap'd one out of the table.
2 GENT. ' Thou shalt not steal ' ?   10
LUCIO. Ay, that he raz'd.
1 GENT. Why, 'twas a commandment to command the captain and
    all the rest from their functions : they put torth to steal.   There's
    not a soldier of us all that, in the thanksgiving before meat, do
    relish the petition well that prays for peace.   16
2 GENT. I never heard any soldier dislike it.
LUCIO. I believe thee ; for I think thou never wast where grace was
    said.
2 GENT. No ?   A dozen times at least.   20
1 GENT. What, in metre ?
LUCIO. In any proportion or in any language.
1 GENT. I think, or in any religion.
LUCIO. Ay, why not ?   Grace is grace, despite of all controversy ; as,
    for example, thou thyself art a wicked villain, despite of all grace.
1 GENT. Well, there went but a pair of shears between us.
LUCIO. I grant ; as there may between the lists and the velvet.
    Thou art the list.   30
1 GENT. And thou the velvet ; thou art good velvet ; thou'rt a
    three-pil'd piece, I warrant thee.   I had as lief be a list of an
    English kersey as be pil'd, as thou art pil'd, for a French velvet.
    Do I speak feelingly now ?
LUCIO. I think thou dost ; and, indeed, with most painful feeling of
    thy speech.   I will, out of thine own confession, learn to begin
    thy health ; but, whilst I live, forget to drink after thee.
1 GENT. I think I have done myself wrong, have I not ?   40
2 GENT. Yes, that thou hast, whether thou art tainted or free.

SCENE 2
Interior. A Brothel.
Day.

Enter MISTRESS OVERDONE.

LUCIO. Behold, behold, where Madam Mitigation comes! I have
purchas'd as many diseases under her roof as come to— 45
2 GENT. To what, I pray?
1 GENT. Judge.
2 GENT. To three thousand dolours a year.
1 GENT. Ay, and more.
LUCIO. A French crown more. 50
1 GENT. Thou art always figuring diseases in me. but thou art full
of error; I am sound.
LUCIO. Nay, not, as one would say, healthy; but so sound as things
that are hollow: thy bones are hollow; impiety has made a
feast of thee. 55
1 GENT. How now! which of your hips has the most profound
sciatica?
MRS. OV. Well, well! there's one yonder arrested and carried to
prison was worth five thousand of you all.
1 GENT. Who's that, I pray thee? 60
MRS. OV. Marry, sir, that's Claudio, Signior Claudio.
1 GENT. Claudio to prison 'Tis not so.
MRS. OV. Nay, but I know 'tis so: I saw him arrested; saw him
carried away; and, which is more, within these three days his
head to be chopp'd off. 65
LUCIO. But, after all this fooling, I would not have it so. Art thou
sure of this?
MRS. OV. I am too sure of it; and it is for getting Madam Julietta
with child.
LUCIO. Believe me, this may be; he promis'd to meet me two hours
since, and he was ever precise in promise-keeping. 72
2 GENT. Besides, you know. it draws something near to the speech
we had to such a purpose.
1 GENT. But most of all agreeing with the proclamation.
LUCIO. Away; let's go learn the truth of it.
[*exeunt* LUCIO *and* GENTLEMEN.
MRS. OV. Thus, what with the war, what with the sweat, what with
the gallows, and what with poverty, I am custom-shrunk. 80

Enter POMPEY.

How now! what's the news with you?
POM. Yonder man is carried to prison.
MRS. OV. Well, what has he done?
POM. A woman.
MRS. OV. But what's his offence? 85
POM. Groping for trouts in a peculiar river.
MRS. OV. What! is there a maid with child by him?
POM. No; but there's a woman with maid by him. You have not
heard of the proclamation, have you?
MRS. OV. What proclamation, man? 90
POM. All houses in the suburbs of Vienna must be pluck'd down.
MRS. OV. And what shall become of those in the city?
POM. They shall stand for seed; they had gone down too, but
that a wise burgher put in for them. 95
MRS. OV. But shall all our houses of resort in the suburbs be pull'd
down?

Lines 46-55 omitted.

32

Kenneth Colley as the Duke and Kevin Stoney as Escalus

John McEnery as Lucio

Adrienne Corri as Mistress Overdone

The Duke (Kenneth Colley) and Claudio (Christopher Strauli)

POM. To the ground, mistress.
MRS. OV. Why, here's a change indeed in the commonwealth!
  What shall become of me?   100
POM. Come, fear not you : good counsellors lack no clients. Though
  you change your place you need not change your trade ; I'll be
  your tapster still. Courage, there will be pity taken on you ;
  you that have worn your eyes almost out in the service, you will
  be considered.   105
MRS. OV. What's to do here, Thomas Tapster ? Let's withdraw.
POM. Here comes Signior Claudio, led by the provost to prison ;
  and there's Madam Juliet.   [exeunt.

Enter PROVOST, CLAUDIO, JULIET, *and* OFFICERS ; LUCIO *following.*

CLAUD. Fellow, why dost thou show me thus to th' world ?   110
  Bear me to prison, where I am committed.
PROV. I do it not in evil disposition,
  But from Lord Angelo by special charge.
CLAUD. Thus can the demigod Authority
  Make us pay down for our offence by weight   115
  The words of heaven : on whom it will, it will ;
  On whom it will not, so ; yet still 'tis just.
LUCIO. Why, how now, Claudio, whence comes this restraint ?
CLAUD. From too much liberty, my Lucio, liberty ;
  As surfeit is the father of much fast,   120
  So every scope by the immoderate use
  Turns to restraint. Our natures do pursue,
  Like rats that ravin down their proper bane,
  A thirsty evil ; and when we drink we die.
LUCIO. If I could speak so wisely under an arrest, I would send for
  certain of my creditors ; and yet, to say the truth, I had as lief
  have the foppery of freedom as the morality of imprisonment.
  What's thy offence, Claudio ?
CLAUD. What but to speak of would offend again.
LUCIO. What, is't murder ?   130
CLAUD. No.
LUCIO. Lechery ?
CLAUD. Call it so.
PROV. Away, sir ; you must go.
CLAUD. One word, good friend. Lucio, a word with you.   135
LUCIO. A hundred, if they'll do you any good. Is lechery so look'd
  after ?
CLAUD. Thus stands it with me : upon a true contract
  I got possession of Julietta's bed.
  You know the lady ; she is fast my wife,   140
  Save that we do the denunciation lack
  Of outward order ; this we came not to,
  Only for propagation of a dow'r
  Remaining in the coffer of her friends,
  From whom we thought it meet to hide our love   145
  Till time had made them for us. But it chances
  The stealth of our most mutual entertainment,
  With character too gross, is writ on Juliet.
LUCIO. With child, perhaps ?
CLAUD.   Unhappily, even so.

'What's to do here . . .
Madam Juliet'
omitted.

SCENE 3
Exterior. Street. Night.

And the new deputy now for the Duke— 150
Whether it be the fault and glimpse of newness,
Or whether that the body public be
A horse whereon the governor doth ride,
Who, newly in the seat, that it may know
He can command, lets it straight feel the spur; 155
Whether the tyranny be in his place,
Or in his eminence that fills it up,
I stagger in. But this new governor
Awakes me all the enrolled penalties
Which have, like unscour'd armour, hung by th' wall 160
So long that nineteen zodiacs have gone round
And none of them been worn ; and, for a name,
Now puts the drowsy and neglected act
Freshly on me. 'Tis surely for a name.

LUCIO. I warrant it is ; and thy head stands so tickle on thy shoulders
    that a milkmaid, if she be in love, may sigh it off.
    Send after the Duke, and appeal to him.

CLAUD. I have done so, but he's not to be found.
    I prithee, Lucio, do me this kind service :
    This day my sister should the cloister enter, 170
    And there receive her approbation ;
    Acquaint her with the danger of my state ;
    Implore her, in my voice, that she make friends
    To the strict deputy ; bid herself assay him.
    I have great hope in that ; for in her youth 175
    There is a prone and speechless dialect
    Such as move men ; beside, she hath prosperous art
    When she will play with reason and discourse,
    And well she can persuade.

LUCIO. I pray she may ; as well for the encouragement of the like,
    which else would stand under grievous imposition, as for the
    enjoying of thy life, who I would be sorry should be thus foolishly
    lost at a game of tick-tack. I'll to her.

CLAUD. I thank you, good friend Lucio. 185

LUCIO. Within two hours.

CLAUD. Come, officer, away. [*exeunt.*

SCENE 4
*Exterior. The Prison
Gates. Night.*
LUCIO, CLAUDIO

Lines 186–187
omitted.

SCENE III. *A monastery.*

Enter DUKE *and* FRIAR THOMAS.

DUKE. No, holy father ; throw away that thought ;
Believe not that the dribbling dart of love
Can pierce a complete bosom. Why I desire thee
To give me secret harbour hath a purpose
More grave and wrinkled than the aims and ends 5
Of burning youth.

FRI.   May your Grace speak of it ?

DUKE. My holy sir, none better knows than you
How I have ever lov'd the life removed,
And held in idle price to haunt assemblies
Where youth, and cost, a witless bravery keeps. 10

SCENE 5
*Exterior. The Cloisters
of a Monastery. Day.*

I have deliver'd to Lord Angelo,
A man of stricture and firm abstinence,
My absolute power and place here in Vienna,
And he supposes me travell'd to Poland ;
For so I have strew'd it in the common ear,   15
And so it is received.   Now, pious sir,
You will demand of me why I do this.
FRI. Gladly, my lord.
DUKE. We have strict statutes and most biting laws,
The needful bits and curbs to headstrong steeds,   20
Which for this fourteen years we have let slip ;
Even like an o'ergrown lion in a cave,
That goes not out to prey.   Now, as fond fathers,
Having bound up the threat'ning twigs of birch,
Only to stick it in their children's sight   25
For terror, not to use, in time the rod
Becomes more mock'd than fear'd ; so our decrees,
Dead to infliction, to themselves are dead ;
And liberty plucks justice by the nose ;
The baby beats the nurse, and quite athwart   30
Goes all decorum.
FRI.   It rested in your Grace
To unloose this tied-up justice when you pleas'd ;
And it in you more dreadful would have seem'd
Than in Lord Angelo.
DUKE.   I do fear, too dreadful.
Sith 'twas my fault to give the people scope,   35
'Twould be my tyranny to strike and gall them
For what I bid them do ; for we bid this be done,
When evil deeds have their permissive pass
And not the punishment.   Therefore, indeed, my father,
I have on Angelo impos'd the office ;   40
Who may, in th' ambush of my name, strike home,
And yet my nature never in the fight
To do in slander.   And to behold his sway,
I will, as 'twere a brother of your order,
Visit both prince and people.   Therefore, I prithee,   45
Supply me with the habit, and instruct me
How I may formally in person bear me
Like a true friar.   Moe reasons for this action
At our more leisure shall I render you.
Only, this one : Lord Angelo is precise ;   50
Stands at a guard with envy ; scarce confesses
That his blood flows, or that his appetite
Is more to bread than stone.   Hence shall we see,
If power change purpose, what our seemers be.   [*exeunt.*

SCENE IV. *A nunnery.*

Enter ISABELLA *and* FRANCISCA.

ISAB. And have you nuns no farther privileges ?
FRAN. Are not these large enough ?
ISAB. Yes, truly ; I speak not as desiring more,
But rather wishing a more strict restraint

SCENE 6
*Exterior. The Courtyard
of a Nunnery. Day.*

Upon the sisterhood, the votarists of Saint Clare.   5
LUCIO. [*Within*] Ho! Peace be in this place!
ISAB.   Who's that which calls?
FRAN. It is a man's voice. Gentle Isabella,
Turn you the key, and know his business of him
You may, I may not; you are yet unsworn;
When you have vow'd, you must not speak with men   10
But in the presence of the prioress;
Then, if you speak, you must not show your face,
Or, if you show your face, you must not speak.
He calls again; I pray you answer him.   [*exit* FRANCISCA.
ISAB. Peace and prosperity! Who is't that calls?   15

                    Enter LUCIO. | LUCIO *does not enter.*

LUCIO. Hail, virgin, if you be, as those cheek-roses
Proclaim you are no less. Can you so stead me
As bring me to the sight of Isabella,
A novice of this place, and the fair sister
To her unhappy brother Claudio?   20
ISAB. Why her ' unhappy brother'? Let me ask
The rather, for I now must make you know
I am that Isabella, and his sister.
LUCIO. Gentle and fair, your brother kindly greets you.
Not to be weary with you, he's in prison.   25   ISABELLA *opens the door*
ISAB. Woe me! For what?   *and* LUCIO *enters.*
LUCIO. For that which, if myself might be his judge,
He should receive his punishment in thanks:
He hath got his friend with child.
ISAB. Sir, make me not your story.
LUCIO.   It is true.   30
I would not—though 'tis my familiar sin
With maids to seem the lapwing, and to jest,
Tongue far from heart—play with all virgins so.
I hold you as a thing enskied and sainted,
By your renouncement an immortal spirit,   35
And to be talk'd with in sincerity,
As with a saint.
ISAB. You do blaspheme the good in mocking me.
LUCIO. Do not believe it. Fewness and truth, 'tis thus.
Your brother and his lover have embrac'd.
As those that feed grow full, as blossoming time   40
That from the seedness the bare fallow brings
To teeming foison, even so her plenteous womb
Expresseth his full tilth and husbandry.
ISAB. Some one with child by him? My cousin Juliet?   45
LUCIO. Is she your cousin?
ISAB. Adoptedly, as school-maids change their names
By vain though apt affection.
LUCIO.   She it is.
ISAB. O, let him marry her!
LUCIO.   This is the point.
The Duke is very strangely gone from hence;   50
Bore many gentlemen, myself being one

36

In hand, and hope of action ; but we do learn,
By those that know the very nerves of state,
His givings-out were of an infinite distance
From his true-meant design.   Upon his place,   55
And with full line of his authority,
Governs Lord Angelo, a man whose blood
Is very snow-broth, one who never feels
The wanton stings and motions of the sense,
But doth rebate and blunt his natural edge   60
With profits of the mind, study and fast.
He—to give fear to use and liberty,
Which have for long run by the hideous law,
As mice by lions—hath pick'd out an act
Under whose heavy sense your brother's life   65
Falls into forfeit ; he arrests him on it,
And follows close the rigour of the statute
To make him an example.   All hope is gone,
Unless you have the grace by your fair prayer
To soften Angelo.   And that's my pith of business   70
'Twixt you and your poor brother.
ISAB. Doth he so seek his life ?
LUCIO.   Has censur'd him
Already, and, as I hear, the Provost hath
A warrant for his execution.
ISAB. Alas !   what poor ability's in me   75
To do him good ?
LUCIO.   Assay the pow'r you have.
ISAB. My power, alas, I doubt !
LUCIO.   Our doubts are traitors,
And make us lose the good we oft might win
By fearing to attempt.   Go to Lord Angelo,
And let him learn to know, when maidens sue,   80
Men give like gods ; but when they weep and kneel,
All their petitions are as freely theirs
As they themselves would owe them.
ISAB. I'll see what I can do.
LUCIO.   But speedily.
ISAB. I will about it straight ;   85
No longer staying but to give the Mother
Notice of my affair.   I humbly thank you.
Commend me to my brother ;   soon at night
I'll send him certain word of my success.
LUCIO. I take my leave of you.
ISAB.   Good sir, adieu.   [*exeunt.*

ACT TWO.

SCENE I.   *A hall in Angelo's house.*

Enter ANGELO, ESCALUS, *a* JUSTICE, PROVOST, OFFICERS, *and other* ATTENDANTS.

ANG. We must not make a scarecrow of the law,
Setting it up to fear the birds of prey,

SCENE 7
*Interior. The Duke's
Audience Chamber.
Night.*

And let it keep one shape till custom make it
Their perch, and not their terror.
ESCAL.   Ay, but yet
  Let us be keen, and rather cut a little   5
  Than fall and bruise to death.   Alas ! this gentleman,
  Whom I would save, had a most noble father.
  Let but your honour know,
  Whom I believe to be most strait in virtue,
  That, in the working of your own affections,   10
  Had time coher'd with place, or place with wishing,
  Or that the resolute acting of our blood
  Could have attain'd th' effect of your own purpose,
  Whether you had not sometime in your life
  Err'd in this point which now you censure him,   15
  And pull'd the law upon you.
ANG. 'Tis one thing to be tempted, Escalus,
  Another thing to fall.   I not deny
  The jury, passing on the prisoner's life,
  May in the sworn twelve have a thief or two   20
  Guiltier than him they try.   What's open made to justice,
  That justice seizes.   What knows the laws
  That thieves do pass on thieves ? 'Tis very pregnant,
  The jewel that we find, we stoop and take't,
  Because we see it ; but what we do not see   25
  We tread upon, and never think of it.
  You may not so extenuate his offence
  For I have had such faults ; but rather tell me,
  When I, that censure him, do so offend,
  Let mine own judgment pattern out my death,   30
  And nothing come in partial.   Sir, he must die.
ESCAL. Be it as your wisdom will.
ANG.   Where is the Provost ?
PROV. Here, if it like your honour.
ANG.   See that Claudio
  Be executed by nine to-morrow morning ;
  Bring him his confessor ; let him be prepar'd ;   35
  For that's the utmost of his pilgrimage.   [exit PROVOST.
ESCAL. [aside.]   Well, heaven forgive him ! and forgive us all !
  Some rise by sin, and some by virtue fall ;
  Some run from breaks of ice, and answer none,
  And some condemned for a fault alone.   40

          Enter ELBOW *and* OFFICERS *with* FROTH *and* POMPEY.

ELB. Come, bring them away ; if these be good people in a common-   'Come, bring . . .
  weal that do nothing but use their abuses in common houses, I   bring them away'
  know no law ; bring them away.   omitted.
ANG. How now, sir ! What's your name, and what's the matter ?   45
ELB. If it please your honour, I am the poor Duke's constable, and
  my name is Elbow ; I do lean upon justice, sir, and do bring in
  here before your good honour two notorious benefactors.
ANG. Benefactors ! Well—what benefactors are they ? Are they not
  malefactors ?   51
ELB. If it please your honour, I know not well what they are ; but
  precise villains they are, that I am sure of, and void of all pro-

                                    38

fanation in the world that good Christians ought to have.   55

ESCAL. This comes off well ; here's a wise officer.

ANG. Go to ; what quality are they of ? Elbow is your name ? Why
dost thou not speak, Elbow ?

POM. He cannot, sir ; he's out at elbow.

ANG. What are you, sir ?   60

ELB. He, sir ? A tapster, sir ; parcelbawd ; one that serves a bad
woman ; whose house, sir, was, as they say, pluck'd down in the
suburbs ; and now she professes a hot-house, which, I think, is a
very ill house too.

ESCAL. How know you that ?   65

ELB. My wife, sir, whom I detest before heaven and your honour—

ESCAL. How ! thy wife !

ELB. Ay, sir ; whom I thank heaven, is an honest woman—

ESCAL. Dost thou detest her therefore ?

ELB. I say, sir, I will detest myself also, as well as she, that this house,
if it be not a bawd's house, it is pity of her life, for it is a naughty
house.

ESCAL. How dost thou know that, constable ?   75

ELB. Marry, sir, by my wife ; who, if she had been a woman cardinally
given, might have been accus'd in fornication, adultery, and all
uncleanliness there.

ESCAL. By the woman's means ?

ELB. Ay, sir, by Mistress Overdone's means ; but as she spit in his
face, so she defied him.   81

POM. Sir, if it please your honour, this is not so.

ELB. Prove it before these varlets here, thou honourable man, prove it.

ESCAL. Do you hear how he misplaces ?

POM. Sir, she came in great with child ; and longing, saving your
honour's reverence, for stew'd prunes. Sir, we had but two in
the house, which at that very distant time stood, as it were, in a
fruit dish, a dish of some three pence ; your honours have seen
such dishes ; they are not China dishes, but very good dishes. 91

ESCAL. Go to, go to ; no matter for the dish, sir.

POM. No, indeed, sir, not of a pin ; you are therein in the right;
but to the point. As I say, this Mistress Elbow, being, as I say,
with child, and being great-bellied, and longing, as I said, for
prunes ; and having but two in the dish, as I said, Master Froth
here, this very man, having eaten the rest, as I said, and, as I say,
paying for them very honestly ; for, as you know, Master Froth,
I could not give you three pence again—   100

FROTH. No, indeed.

POM. Very well ; you being then, if you be rememb'red, cracking the
stones of the foresaid prunes—

FROTH. Ay, so I did indeed.

POM. Why, very well ; I telling you then, if you be rememb'red, that
such a one and such a one were past cure of the thing you wot of,
unless they kept very good diet, as I told you—

FROTH. All this is true.

POM. Why, very well then—   110

ESCAL. Come, you are a tedious fool. To the purpose : what was
done to Elbow's wife that he hath cause to complain of ? Come
me to what was done to her.

POM. Sir, your honour cannot come to that yet.

'not of a pin . . . for prunes' omitted.

'Ay, so I did . . . very well then' omitted.

ESCAL. No, sir, nor I mean it not.   115
POM. Sir, but you shall come to it, by your honour's leave.   And, I
  beseech you, look into Master Froth here, sir, a man of fourscore
  pound a year ; whose father died at Hallowmas—was't not at
  Hallowmas, Master Froth ?
FROTH. All-hallond eve.   120
POM. Why, very well ; I hope here be truths.   He, sir, sitting, as I
  say, in a lower chair, sir , 'twas in the Bunch of Grapes, where,
  indeed, you have a delight to sit, have you not ?
FROTH. I have so ; because it is an open room, and good for winter.
POM. Why, very well then ; I hope here be truths.
ANG. This will last out a night in Russia,
  When nights are longest there ; I'll take my leave,
  And leave you to the hearing of the cause,   130
  Hoping you'll find good cause to whip them all.
ESCAL. I think no less.   Good morrow to your lordship.
                                               [exit ANGELO.
  Now, sir, come on ; what was done to Elbow's wife, once more ?
POM. Once ?—sir.   There was nothing done to her once.
ELB. I beseech you, sir, ask him what this man did to my wife.   136
POM. I beseech your honour, ask me.
ESCAL. Well, sir, what did this gentleman to her ?
POM. I beseech you, sir, look in this gentleman's face.   Good Master
  Froth, look upon his honour ; 'tis for a good purpose.   Doth your
  honour mark his face ?
ESCAL. Ay, sir, very well.
POM. Nay, I beseech you, mark it well.
ESCAL. Well, I do so.   145
POM. Doth your honour see any harm in his face ?
ESCAL. Why, no.
POM. I'll be suppos'd upon a book his face is the worst thing about
  him.   Good then ; if his face be the worst thing about him, how
  could Master Froth do the constable's wife any harm ?   I would
  know that of your honour.   152
ESCAL. He's in the right, constable ; what say you to it ?
ELB. First, an it like you, the house is a respected house ; next, this
  is a respected fellow ; and his mistress is a respected woman.
POM. By this hand, sir, his wife is a more respected person than any
  of us all.
ELB. Varlet, thou liest ; thou liest, wicket varlet ; the time is yet to
  come that she was ever respected with man, woman, or child.   161
POM. Sir, she was respected with him before he married with her.
ESCAL. Which is the wiser here, Justice or Iniquity ?   Is this true ?
ELB. O thou caitiff !   O thou varlet !   O thou wicked Hannibal !   I
  respected with her before I was married to her !   If ever I was
  respected with her, or she with me, let not your worship think
  me the poor Duke's officer.   Prove this, thou wicked Hannibal,
  or I'll have mine action of batt'ry on thee.   171
ESCAL. If he took you a box o' th' ear, you might have your action of
  slander too.
ELB. Marry, I thank your good worship for it.   What is't your worship's pleasure I shall do with this wicked caitiff ?   176
ESCAL. Truly, officer, because he hath some offences in him that thou

'Why, very well . . .
here be truths'
omitted.

'with man, woman, or
child . . . Duke's
officer' omitted.

wouldst discover if thou couldst, let him continue in his courses
till thou know'st what they are.

ELB. Marry, I thank your worship for it.   Thou seest, thou wicked
varlet, now, what's come upon thee : thou art to continue now,
thou varlet ; thou art to continue.

ESCAL. Where were you born, friend ?

FROTH. Here in Vienna, sir.

ESCAL. Are you of fourscore pounds a year ?   185

FROTH. Yes, an't please you, sir

ESCAL. So.   What trade are you of, sir ?

POM. A tapster, a poor widow's tapster.

ESCAL. Your mistress' name ?

POM. Mistress Overdone.   190

ESCAL. Hath she had any more than one husband ?

POM. Nine, sir ; Overdone by the last.

ESCAL. Nine ! Come hither to me, Master Froth.   Master Froth, I
would not have you acquainted with tapsters : they will draw
you, Master Froth, and you will hang them.   Get you gone, and
let me hear no more of you.   196

FROTH. I thank your worship.   For mine own part, I never come into
any room in a taphouse but I am drawn in.

ESCAL. Well, no more of it, Master Froth ; farewell. [exit FROTH.]
Come you hither to me, Master Tapster ; what's your name,
Master Tapster.

POM. Pompey.

ESCAL. What else ?

POM. Bum, sir.   205

ESCAL. Troth, and your bum is the greatest thing about you ; so
that, in the beastliest sense, you are Pompey the Great.   Pompey,
you are partly a bawd, Pompey, howsoever you colour it in being
a tapster.   Are you not ? Come, tell me true ; it shall be the
better for you.   210

POM. Truly, sir, I am a poor fellow that would live.

ESCAL. How would you live, Pompey—by being a bawd ? What do
you think of the trade, Pompey ? Is it a lawful trade ?

POM. If the law would allow it, sir.   215

ESCAL. But the law will not allow it, Pompey ; nor it shall not be
allowed in Vienna.

POM. Does your worship mean to geld and splay all the youth of the
city ?

ESCAL. No, Pompey.   220

POM. Truly, sir, in my poor opinion, they will to't then.   If your
worship will take order for the drabs and the knaves, you need
not to fear the bawds.

ESCAL. There is pretty orders beginning, I can tell you : but it is but
heading and hanging.   225

POM. If you head and hang all that offend that way but for ten year
together, you'll be glad to give out a commission for more heads ;
if this law hold in Vienna ten year, I'll rent the fairest house in it,
after threepence a bay.   If you live to see this come to pass, say
Pompey told you so.   231

ESCAL. Thank you, good Pompey ; and, in requital of your prophecy,
hark you ; I advise you, let me not find you before me again upon
any complaint whatsoever—no, not for dwelling where you do ;

if I do, Pompey, I shall beat you to your tent, and prove a shrewd
Cæsar to you ; in plain dealing, Pompey, I shall have you whipt.
So for this time, Pompey, fare you well.   238
POM. I thank your worship for your good counsel ; [*aside*] but I
   shall follow it as the flesh and fortune shall better determine.
   Whip me ? No, no ; let carman whip his jade ;
   The valiant heart's not whipt out of his trade.   [*exit.*
ESCAL. Come hither to me, Master Elbow ; come hither, Master
   Constable. How long have you been in this place of constable ?
ELB. Seven year and a half, sir.   247
ESCAL. I thought, by the readiness in the office, you had continued
   in it some time. You say seven years together ?
ELB. And a half, sir.
ESCAL. Alas, it hath been great pains to you ! They do you wrong to
   put you so oft upon't. Are there not men in your ward sufficient
   to serve it ?   254
ELB. Faith, sir, few of any wit in such matters ; as they are chosen,
   they are glad to choose me for them ; I do it for some piece of
   money, and go through with all.
ESCAL. Look you, bring me in the names of some six or seven, the
   most sufficient of your parish.
ELB. To your worship's house, sir ?   260
ESCAL. To my house. Fare you well. [*exit* ELBOW.] What's
   o'clock, think you ?
JUST. Eleven, sir.
ESCAL. I pray you home to dinner with me.
JUST. I humbly thank you.   265
ESCAL. It grieves me for the death of Claudio ;
   But there's no remedy.
JUST. Lord Angelo is severe.
ESCAL.   It is but needful :
   Mercy is not itself that oft looks so ;
   Pardon is still the nurse of second woe.   270
   But yet, poor Claudio ! There is no remedy.
   Come, sir.   [*exeunt.*

'What's o'clock, think
you' omitted.
'Eleven, sir' omitted.

'There is no remedy.
Come, sir' omitted.

SCENE II *Another room in Angelo's house.*

Enter PROVOST *and a* SERVANT.

SERV. He's hearing of a cause ; he will come straight.
   I'll tell him of you.
PROV. Pray you do.   [*exit* SERVANT.
   I'll know
   His pleasure ; may be he will relent. Alas,
   He hath but as offended in a dream !
   All sects, all ages, smack of this vice ; and he   5
   To die for 't !

Enter ANGELO.

ANG.   Now, what's the matter, Provost ?
PROV. Is it your will Claudio shall die to-morrow ?
ANG. Did not I tell thee yea ? Hadst thou not order ?
   Why dost thou ask again ?
PROV.   Lest I might be too rash ;

SCENE 8
*Interior. The Duke's
Audience Chamber.
Night.*
ANGELO, PROVOST.

Lines 1–6 omitted.

Under your good correction, I have seen   10
When, after execution, judgment hath
Repented o'er his doom.
ANG.   Go to ; let that be mine.
Do you your office, or give up your place,
And you shall well be spar'd.
PROV.   I crave your honour's pardon.
What shall be done, sir, with the groaning Juliet ?   15
She's very near her hour.
ANG.   Dispose of her
To some more fitter place, and that with speed.

Re-enter SERVANT.
SERV. Here is the sister of the man condemn'd
Desires access to you.
ANG.   Hath he a sister ?
PROV. Ay, my good lord ; a very virtuous maid,   20
And to be shortly of a sisterhood,
If not already.
ANG.   Well, let her be admitted. [*exit* SERVANT.
See you the fornicatress be remov'd ;
Let her have needful but not lavish means ;
There shall be order for't.
                                                                             Exit PROVOST

Enter LUCIO *and* ISABELLA.

PROV. [*going*] Save your honour ! 25	Line 25 omitted.
ANG. Stay a little while. [*to* ISABELLA] Y'are welcome ; what's your	'Stay a little while'
will ?	omitted.

ISAB. I am a woeful suitor to your honour,
Please but your honour hear me.
ANG.   Well ; what's your suit ?
ISAB. There is a vice that most I do abhor,
And most desire should meet the blow of justice .   30
For which I would not plead, but that I must ;
For which I must not plead, but that I am
At war 'twixt will and will not.
ANG.   Well ; the matter ?
ISAB. I have a brother is condemn'd to die ,
I do beseech you, let it be his fault   35
And not my brother.
| PROV. [*aside.*] Heaven give thee moving graces | 'Heaven give thee |
ANG. Condemn the fault and not the actor of it | moving graces' |
Why, every fault's condemn'd ere it be done | omitted. |
Mine were the very cipher of a function,
To fine the faults whose fine stands in record,   40
And let go by the actor.
ISAB.   O just but severe law
I had a brother, then.   Heaven keep your honour !
LUCIO. [*to* ISABELLA]   Give't not o'er so ; to him again, entreat him,
Kneel down before him, hang upon his gown ,
You are too cold : if you should need a pin,   45
You could not with more tame a tongue desire it.
To him, I say.
ISAB. Must he needs die ?

ANG.   Maiden, no remedy.
ISAB. Yes; I do think that you might pardon him.
   And neither heaven nor man grieve at the mercy.   50
ANG. I will not do't.
ISAB.   But can you, if you would?
ANG. Look, what I will not, that I cannot do.
ISAB. But might you do't, and do the world no wrong,
   If so your heart were touch'd with that remorse
   As mine is to him?
ANG.   He's sentenc'd; 'tis too late.   55
LUCIO. [to ISABELLA] You are too cold.
ISAB. Too late? Why, no; I, that do speak a word,
   May call it back again.   Well, believe this:
   No ceremony that to great ones longs,
   Not the king's crown nor the deputed sword,   60
   The marshal's truncheon nor the judge's robe,
   Become them with one half so good a grace
   As mercy does.
   If he had been as you, and you as he,
   You would have slipp'd like him; but he, like you,   65
   Would not have been so stern.
   ANG.   Pray you be gone.
ISAB. I would to heaven I had your potency,
   And you were Isabel! Should it then be thus?
   No; I would tell what 'twere to be a judge
   And what a prisoner.
LUCIO. [to ISABELLA] Ay, touch him; there's the vein.   70
ANG. Your brother is a forfeit of the law,
   And you but waste your words.
   ISAB.   Alas! Alas!
   Why, all the souls that were were forfeit once;
   And He that might the vantage best have took
   Found out the remedy.   How would you be   75
   If He, which is the top of judgment, should
   But judge you as you are? O think on that;
   And mercy then will breathe within your lips,
   Like man new made.
ANG.   Be you content, fair maid.
   It is the law, not I condemn your brother.   80
   Were he my kinsman, brother, or my son,
   It should be thus with him.   He must die to-morrow.
ISAB. To-morrow! O, that's sudden! Spare him, spare him.
   He's not prepar'd for death.   Even for our kitchens
   We kill the fowl of season; shall we serve heaven   85
   With less respect than we do minister
   To our gross selves? Good, good my lord, bethink you.
   Who is it that hath died for this offence?
   There's many have committed it.
LUCIO. [aside]   Ay, well said.
ANG. The law hath not been dead, though it hath slept.   90
   Those many had not dar'd to do that evil
   If the first that did th' edict infringe
   Had answer'd for his deed.   Now 'tis awake,
   Takes note of what is done, and, like a prophet,

Looks in a glass that shows what future evils—   95
Either now or by remissness new conceiv'd,
And so in progress to be hatch'd and born—
Are now to have no successive degrees,
But here they live to end.
ISAB.   Yet show some pity.
ANG. I show it most of all when I show justice;   100
For then I pity those I do not know,
Which a dismiss'd offence would after gall,
And do him right that, answering one foul wrong,
Lives not to act another.   Be satisfied;
Your brother dies to-morrow; be content.   105
ISAB. So you must be the first that gives this sentence,
And he that suffers.   O, it is excellent
To have a giant's strength! But it is tyrannous
To use it like a giant.
LUCIO. [to ISABELLA] That's well said.
ISAB. Could great men thunder   110
As Jove himself does, Jove would never be quiet,
For every pelting petty officer
Would use his heaven for thunder,
Nothing but thunder.   Merciful Heaven,
Thou rather, with thy sharp and sulphurous bolt,   115
Splits the unwedgeable and gnarled oak
Than the soft myrtle.   But man, proud man,
Dress'd in a little brief authority,
Most ignorant of what he's most assur'd,
His glassy essence, like an angry ape,   120
Plays such fantastic tricks before high heaven
As makes the angels weep; who, with our spleens,
Would all themselves laugh mortal.
LUCIO. [to ISABELLA] O, to him, to him, wench! He will relent;
He's coming; I perceive 't.
PROV. [aside] Pray heaven she win him.   125
ISAB. We cannot weigh our brother with ourself.
Great men may jest with saints: 'tis wit in them;
But in the less foul profanation.
LUCIO. [to ISABELLA] Thou'rt i' th' right, girl; more o' that.
ISAB. That in the captain's but a choleric word   130
Which in the soldier is flat blasphemy.
LUCIO. [to ISABELLA] Art avis'd o' that? More on't.
ANG. Why do you put these sayings upon me?
ISAB. Because authority, though it err like others,
Hath yet a kind of medicine in itself   135
That skins the vice o' th' top.   Go to your bosom,
Knock there, and ask your heart what it doth know
That's like my brother's fault.   If it confess
A natural guiltiness such as is his,
Let it not sound a thought upon your tongue   140
Against my brother's life.
ANG. [aside]   She speaks, and 'tis
Such sense that my sense breeds with it.—Fare you well.
ISAB. Gentle my lord, turn back.
ANG. I will bethink me.   Come again to-morrow.

ISAB. Hark how I'll bribe you ; good my lord, turn back.   145
ANG. How, bribe me ?
ISAB. Ay, with such gifts that heaven shall share with you.
| LUCIO. [to ISABELLA] You had marr'd all else. | Line 148 omitted.
ISAB. Not with fond sicles of the tested gold,
    Or stones, whose rate are either rich or poor   150
    As fancy values them ; but with true prayers
    That shall be up at heaven and enter there
    Ere sun-rise, prayers from preserved souls,
    From fasting maids, whose minds are dedicate
    To nothing temporal.
ANG.   Well ; come to me to-morrow.   155
LUCIO. [to ISABELLA] Go to : 'tis well ; away.
ISAB. Heaven keep your honour safe !
ANG.   [aside] Amen ; for I
    Am that way going to temptation
    Where prayers cross.
ISAB.   At what hour to-morrow
    Shall I attend your lordship ?
ANG.   At any time 'fore noon.   160
ISAB. Save your honour !   [exeunt all but ANGELO.
ANG.   From thee ; even from thy virtue !
    What's this, what's this ? Is this her fault or mine ?
    The tempter or the tempted, who sins most ?
    Ha !
    Not she ; nor doth she tempt ; but it is I   165
    That, lying by the violet in the sun,
    Do as the carrion does, not as the flow'r,
    Corrupt with virtuous season. Can it be
    That modesty may more betray our sense
    Than woman's lightness ? Having waste ground enough,   170
    Shall we desire to raze the sanctuary,
    And pitch our evils there ? O, fie, fie, fie !
    What dost thou, or what art thou, Angelo ?
    Dost thou desire her foully for those things
    That make her good ? O, let her brother live !   175
    Thieves for their robbery have authority
    When judges steal themselves. What, do I love her,
    That I desire to hear her speak again,
    And feast upon her eyes ? What is't I dream on ?
    O cunning enemy, that, to catch a saint,   180
    With saints dost bait thy hook ! Most dangerous
    Is that temptation that doth goad us on
    To sin in loving virtue. Never could the strumpet,
    With all her double vigour, art and nature,
    Once stir my temper ; but this virtuous maid   185
    Subdues me quite. Ever till now,
    When men were fond, I smil'd and wond'red how.   [exit.

SCENE III. *A prison.*

Enter, severally, DUKE, *disguised as a* FRIAR, *and* PROVOST.

| DUKE. Hail to you, PROVOST ! so I think you are.
| PROV. I am the Provost. What's your will, good friar ?

SCENE 9
Interior. The Prison.
Night.
| Lines 1-2 omitted.

DUKE. Bound by my charity and my blest order,
  I come to visit the afflicted spirits
  Here in the prison. Do me the common right   5
  To let me see them, and to make me know
  The nature of their crimes, that I may minister
  To them accordingly.
PROV. I would do more than that, if more were needful.

Enter JULIET.

Look, here comes one ; a gentlewoman of mine,   10   For 'here comes one'
  Who, falling in the flaws of her own youth,   read 'here's'.
  Hath blister'd her report. She is with child ;
  And he that got it, sentenc'd—a young man
  More fit to do another such offence
  Than die for this.   15
DUKE. When must he die ?
PROV.   As I do think, to-morrow.
[*to* JULIET] I have provided for you ; stay awhile
  And you shall be conducted.
DUKE. Repent you, fair one, of the sin you carry ?
JULIET. I do ; and bear the shame most patiently.   20
DUKE. I'll teach you how you shall arraign your conscience,
  And try your penitence, if it be sound
  Or hollowly put on.
JULIET.   I'll gladly learn.
DUKE. Love you the man that wrong'd you ?
JULIET. Yes, as I love the woman that wrong'd him.   25
DUKE. So then, it seems, your most offenceful act
  Was mutually committed.
JULIET.   Mutually.
DUKE. Then was your sin of heavier kind than his.
JULIET. I do confess it, and repent it, father.
DUKE. 'Tis meet so, daughter ; but lest you do repent   30
  As that the sin hath brought you to this shame,
  Which sorrow is always toward ourselves, not heaven,
  Showing we would not spare heaven as we love it,
  But as we stand in fear—
JULIET. I do repent me as it is an evil,   35
  And take the shame with joy.
DUKE.   There rest.
  Your partner, as I hear, must die to-morrow,
  And I am going with instruction to him.
  Grace go with you ! Benedicite !   [*exit.*
JULIET. Must die to-morrow ! O, injurious law,   40
  That respites me a life whose very comfort
  Is still a dying horror !
| PROV.   'Tis pity of him.   [*exeunt.* | 'Tis pity of him'
                                          omitted.

SCENE IV. *Angelo's house.*   SCENE 10
                                       Interior. A Chamber in
Enter ANGELO.   *the Duke's Palace. Day.*

ANG. When I would pray and think, I think and pray
  To several subjects. Heaven hath my empty words,

Whilst my invention, hearing not my tongue,
Anchors on Isabel. Heaven in my mouth,
As if I did but only chew his name, 5
And in my heart the strong and swelling evil
Of my conception. The state whereon I studied
Is, like a good thing being often read,
Grown sere and tedious ; yea, my gravity,
Wherein—let no man hear me—I take pride, 10
Could I with boot change for an idle plume
Which the air beats for vain. O place, O form,
How often dost thou with thy case, thy habit,
Wrench awe from fools, and tie the wiser souls
To thy false seeming ! Blood, thou art blood. 15
Let's write 'good angel ' on the devil's horn ;
'Tis not the devil's crest.

Enter SERVANT.

     How now, who's there ?
SERV. One Isabel, a sister, desires access to you.
ANG. Teach her the way. [*exit* SERVANT.] O heavens !
 Why does my blood thus muster to my heart, 20
 Making both it unable for itself
 And dispossessing all my other parts
 Of necessary fitness ?
 So play the foolish throngs with one that swoons ;
 Come all to help him, and so stop the air 25
 By which he should revive ; and even so
 The general subject to a well-wish'd king
 Quit their own part, and in obsequious fondness
 Crowd to his presence, where their untaught love
 Must needs appear offence.

Enter ISABELLA.

     How now, fair maid ? 30
ISAB. I am come to know your pleasure.
ANG. That you might know it would much better please me
 Than to demand what 'tis. Your brother cannot live.
ISAB. Even so ! Heaven keep your honour !
ANG. Yet may he live awhile, and, it may be, 35
 As long as you or I ; yet he must die.
ISAB. Under your sentence ?
ANG. Yea.
ISAB. When ? I beseech you ; that in his reprieve,
 Longer or shorter, he may be so fitted 40
 That his soul sicken not.
ANG. Ha ! Fie, these filthy vices ! It were as good
 To pardon him that hath from nature stol'n
 A man already made, as to remit
 Their saucy sweetness that do coin heaven's image 45
 In stamps that are forbid ; 'tis all as easy
 Falsely to take away a life true made
 As to put metal in restrained means
 To make a false one.

Lines 26, from 'and
even so', to 30, 'appear
offence', omitted.

SCENE II
*Interior. The Duke's
Audience Chamber.
Day.*
ANGELO, ISABELLA.

48

ISAB. 'Tis set down so in heaven, but not in earth.   50
ANG. Say you so? Then I shall pose you quickly.
   Which had you rather—that the most just law
   Now took your bro:her's life; or, to redeem him
   Give up your body to such sweet uncleanness
   As she that he hath stain'd?
ISAB.   Sir, believe this: 55
   I had rather give my body than my soul.
ANG. I talk not of your soul; our compell'd sins
   Stand more for number than for accompt.
ISAB.   How say you?
ANG. Nay, I'll not warrant that; for I can speak
   Against the thing I say. Answer to this: 60
   I, now the voice of the recorded law,
   Pronounce a sentence on your brother's life;
   Might there not be a charity in sin
   To save this brother's life?
ISAB.   Please you to do't,
   I'll take it as a peril to my soul   65
   It is no sin at all, but charity.
ANG. Pleas'd you to do't at peril of your soul,
   Were equal poise of sin and charity.
ISAB. That I do beg his life, if it be sin,
   Heaven let me bear it! You granting of my suit,   70
   If that be sin, I'll make it my morn prayer
   To have it added to the faults of mine,
   And nothing of your answer.
ANG.   Nay, but hear me;
   Your sense pursues not mine; either you are ignorant
   Or seem so, craftily; and that's not good.   75
ISAB. Let me be ignorant, and in nothing good
   But graciously to know I am no better.
ANG. Thus wisdom wishes to appear most bright
   When it doth tax itself; as these black masks
   Proclaim an enshielded beauty ten times louder   80
   Than beauty could, display'd. But mark me:
   To be received plain, I'll speak more gross—
   Your brother is to die.
ISAB. So.
ANG. And his offence is so, as it appears,   85
   Accountant to the law upon that pain.
ISAB. True.
ANG. Admit no other way to save his life,
   As I subscribe not that, nor any other,
   But, in the loss of question, that you. his sister,   90
   Finding yourself desir'd of such a person
   Whose credit with the judge, or own great place,
   Could fetch your brother from the manacles
   Of the all-binding law; and that there were
   No earthly mean to save him but that either   95
   You must lay down the treasures of your body
   To this supposed, or else to let him suffer—
   What would you do?
ISAB. As much for my poor brother as myself;

49

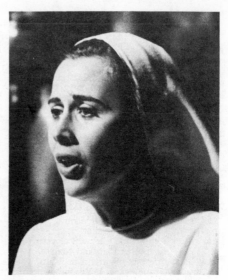

Tim Pigott-Smith as Angelo   *Kate Nelligan as Isabella*

Froth (John Clegg), Pompey (Frank Middlemass) and Elbow (Ellis Jones)

That is, were I under the terms of death,   100
Th' impression of keen whips I'd wear as rubies,
And strip myself to death as to a bed
That longing have been sick for, ere I'd yield
My body up to shame.
ANG.   Then must your brother die.
ISAB. And 'twere the cheaper way :   105
Better it were a brother died at once
Than that a sister, by redeeming him,
Should die for ever.
ANG. Were not you, then, as cruel as the sentence
That you have slander'd so ?   110
ISAB. Ignominy in ransom and free pardon
Are of two houses : lawful mercy
Is nothing kin to foul redemption.
ANG. You seem'd of late to make the law a tyrant ;
And rather prov'd the sliding of your brother   115
A merriment than a vice.
ISAB. O, pardon me, my lord ! It oft falls out,
To have what we would have, we speak not what we mean:
I something do excuse the thing I hate
For his advantage that I dearly love.   120
ANG. We are all frail.
ISAB.   Else let my brother die,
If not a fedary but only he
Owe and succeed thy weakness.
ANG. Nay, women are frail too.
ISAB. Ay, as the glasses where they view themselves,   125
Which are as easy broke as they make forms.
Women, help heaven ! Men their creation mar
In profiting by them.   Nay, call us ten times frail ;
For we are soft as our complexions are,
And credulous to false prints.
ANG.   I think it well ;   130
And from this testimony of your own sex,
Since I suppose we are made to be no stronger
Than faults may shake our frames, let me be bold.
I do arrest your words.   Be that you are,
That is, a woman ; if you be more, you're none ;   135
If you be one, as you are well express'd
By all external warrants, show it now
By putting on the destin'd livery.
ISAB. I have no tongue but one ; gentle, my lord,
Let me intreat you speak the former language.   140
ANG. Plainly conceive, I love you.
ISAB. My brother did love Juliet,
And you tell me that he shall die for't.
ANG. He shall not, Isabel, if you give me love.
ISAB. I know your virtue hath a license in't,   145
Which seems a little fouler than it is,
To pluck on others.
ANG.   Believe me, on mine honour,
My words express my purpose.
ISAB. Ha ! little honour to be much believ'd,

And most pernicious purpose ! Seeming, seeming !   150
I will proclaim thee, Angelo, look for't.
Sign me a present pardon for my brother
Or, with an outstretch'd throat, I'll tell the world aloud
What man thou art.
ANG.   Who will believe thee, Isabel ?
My unsoil'd name, th' austereness of my life,   155
My vouch against you, and my place i' th' state,
Will so your accusation overweigh
That you shall stifle in your own report,
And smell of calumny.   I have begun,
And now I give my sensual race the rein :   160
Fit thy consent to my sharp appetite ;
Lay by all nicety and prolixious blushes
That banish what they sue for ; redeem thy brother
By yielding up thy body to my will ;
Or else he must not only die the death,   165
But thy unkindness shall his death draw out
To ling'ring sufferance.   Answer me to-morrow,
Or, by the affection that now guides me most,
I'll prove a tyrant to him.   As for you,
Say what you can : my false o'erweighs your true.   [*exit.*
ISAB. To whom should I complain ? Did I tell this,   171
Who would believe me ?   O perilous mouths
That bear in them one and the self-same tongue
Either of condemnation or approof,
Bidding the law make curtsy to their will ;   175
Hooking both right and wrong to th' appetite,
To follow as it draws !   I'll to my brother.
Though he hath fall'n by prompture of the blood,
Yet hath he in him such a mind of honour
That, had he twenty heads to tender down   180
On twenty bloody blocks, he'd yield them up
Before his sister should her body stoop
To such abhorr'd pollution.
Then, Isabel, live chaste, and, brother, die :
More than our brother is our chastity.   185
I'll tell him yet of Angelo's request,
And fit his mind to death, for his soul's rest.   [*exit.*

ACT THREE.

SCENE I.   *The prison.*

Enter DUKE, *disguised as before*, CLAUDIO, *and* PROVOST.

DUKE. So, then you hope of pardon from Lord Angelo ?
CLAUD. The miserable have no other medicine
But only hope :
I have hope to live, and am prepar'd to die.
DUKE. Be absolute for death ; either death or life   5
Shall thereby be the sweeter.   Reason thus with life.
If I do lose thee, I do lose a thing

SCENE 12
Interior. The Prison.
Claudio's Cell. Day.

That none but fools would keep.   A breath thou art,
Servile to all the skyey influences,
That dost this habitation where thou keep'st   10
Hourly afflict.   Merely, thou art Death's fool;
For him thou labour'st by thy flight to shun
And yet run'st toward him still.   Thou art not noble;
For all th' accommodations that thou bear'st
Are nurs'd by baseness.   Thou 'rt by no means valiant;   15
For thou dost fear the soft and tender fork
Of a poor worm.   Thy best of rest is sleep,
And that thou oft provok'st; yet grossly fear'st
Thy death, which is no more.   Thou art not thyself;
For thou exists on many a thousand grains   20
That issue out of dust.   Happy thou art not;
For what thou hast not, still thou striv'st to get,
And what thou hast, forget'st.   Thou art not certain;
For thy complexion shifts to strange effects,
After the moon.   If thou art rich, thou'rt poor;   25
For, like an ass whose back with ingots bows,
Thou bear'st thy heavy riches but a journey,
And Death unloads thee.   Friend hast thou none;
For thine own bowels which do call thee sire,
The mere effusion of thy proper loins,   30
Do curse the gout, serpigo, and the rheum,
For ending thee no sooner.   Thou hast nor youth nor age,
But, as it were, an after-dinner's sleep,
Dreaming on both; for all thy blessed youth
Becomes as aged, and doth beg the alms   35
Of palsied eld; and when thou art old and rich,
Thou hast neither heat, affection, limb, nor beauty,
To make thy riches pleasant.   What's yet in this
That bears the name of life?   Yet in this life
Lie hid moe thousand deaths; yet death we fear,   40
That makes these odds all even.
CLAUD.   I humbly thank you.
 To sue to live, I find I seek to die;
 And, seeking death, find life.   Let it come on.
ISAB. [within]   What, ho! Peace here; grace and good company!   Lines 44–50 omitted.
PROV. Who's there? Come in; the wish deserves a welcome.   45
DUKE. Dear sir, ere long I'll visit you again.
CLAUD. Most holy sir, I thank you.

                        Enter ISABELLA.

ISAB. My business is a word or two with Claudio.
PROV. And very welcome.   Look, signior, here's your sister.   50
DUKE. Provost, a word with you.
PROV. As many as you please.
DUKE. Bring me to hear them speak, where I may be conceal'd.
                                [*exeunt* DUKE *and* PROVOST.
CLAUD. Now, sister, what's the comfort?   55
ISAB. Why,
 As all comforts are; most good, most good, indeed.
 Lord Angelo, having affairs to heaven,
 Intends you for his swift ambassador,

    Where you shall be an everlasting leiger.   60
    Therefore, your best appointment make with speed;
    To-morrow you set on.
CLAUD.   Is there no remedy?
ISAB. None, but such remedy as, to save a head,
    To cleave a heart in twain.
CLAUD.   But is there any?
ISAB. Yes, brother, you may live :   65
    There is a devilish mercy in the judge,
    If you'll implore it, that will free your life,
    But fetter you till death.
CLAUD.   Perpetual durance?
ISAB. Ay, just ; perpetual durance, a restraint,
    Though all the world's vastidity you had,   70
    To a determin'd scope.
CLAUD.   But in what nature?
ISAB. In such a one as, you consenting to't,
    Would bark your honour from that trunk you bear,
    And leave you naked.
CLAUD.   Let me know the point.
ISAB. O, I do fear thee, Claudio ; and I quake,   75
    Lest thou a feverous life shouldst entertain,
    And six or seven winters more respect
    Than a perpetual honour. Dar'st thou die?
    The sense of death is most in apprehension ;
    And the poor beetle that we tread upon   80
    In corporal sufferance finds a pang as great
    As when a giant dies.
CLAUD.   Why give you me this shame?
    Think you I can a resolution fetch
    From flow'ry tenderness? If I must die,
    I will encounter darkness as a bride   85
    And hug it in mine arms.
ISAB. There spake my brother ; there my father's grave
    Did utter forth a voice. Yes, thou must die :
    Thou art too noble to conserve a life
    In base appliances. This outward-sainted deputy,   90
    Whose settled visage and deliberate word
    Nips youth i' th' head, and follies doth enew
    As falcon doth the fowl, is yet a devil ;
    His filth within being cast, he would appear
    A pond as deep as hell.
CLAUD.   The precise Angelo!   95
ISAB. O, 'tis the cunning livery of hell
    The damned'st body to invest and cover
    In precise guards ! Dost thou think, Claudio,
    If I would yield him my virginity
    Thou mightst be freed?
CLAUD.   O heavens ! it cannot be.   100
ISAB. Yes, he would give't thee, from this rank offence,
    So to offend him still. This night's the time
    That I should do what I abhor to name,
    Or else thou diest to-morrow.
CLAUD.   Thou shalt not do't.

ISAB. O, were it but my life!   105
　　　I'd throw it down for your deliverance
　　　As frankly as a pin.
CLAUD.   Thanks, dear Isabel.
ISAB. Be ready, Claudio, for your death to-morrow.
CLAUD. Yes.　Has he affections in him
　　　That thus can make him bite the law by th' nose   110
　　　When he would force it?　Sure it is no sin;
　　　Or of the deadly seven it is the least.
ISAB. Which is the least?
CLAUD. If it were damnable, he being so wise,
　　　Why would he for the momentary trick   115
　　　Be perdurably fin'd?—O Isabel!
ISAB. What says my brother?
CLAUD.   Death is a fearful thing.
ISAB. And shamed life a hateful.
CLAUD. Ay, but to die, and go we know not where;
　　　To lie in cold obstruction, and to rot;   120
　　　This sensible warm motion to become
　　　A kneaded clod; and the delighted spirit
　　　To bathe in fiery floods or to reside
　　　In thrilling region of thick-ribbed ice;
　　　To be imprison'd in the viewless winds,   125
　　　And blown with restless violence round about
　　　The pendent world; or to be worse than worst
　　　Of those that lawless and incertain thought
　　　Imagine howling—'tis too horrible.
　　　The weariest and most loathed worldly life   130
　　　That age, ache, penury, and imprisonment,
　　　Can lay on nature is a paradise
　　　To what we fear of death.
ISAB. Alas, alas!
CLAUD.   Sweet sister, let me live.
　　　What sin you do to save a brother's life,   135
　　　Nature dispenses with the deed so far
　　　That it becomes a virtue.
ISAB.   O you beast!
　　　O faithless coward! O dishonest wretch!
　　　Wilt thou be made a man out of my vice?
　　　Is't not a kind of incest to take life   140
　　　From thine own sister's shame? What should I think?
　　　Heaven shield my mother play'd my father fair!
　　　For such a warped slip of wilderness
　　　Ne'er issu'd from his blood.　Take my defiance;
　　　Die; perish.　Might but my bending down   145
　　　Reprieve thee from thy fate, it should proceed.
　　　I'll pray a thousand prayers for thy death,
　　　No word to save thee.
CLAUD. Nay, hear me, Isabel.
ISAB.   O fie, fie, fie!
　　　Thy sin's not accidental, but a trade.   150
　　　Mercy to thee would prove itself a bawd;
　　　'Tis best that thou diest quickly.

CLAUD.   O, hear me. Isabella.

Re-enter DUKE.

DUKE. Vouchsafe a word, young sister, but one word.
ISAB. What is your will ?   154
DUKE. Might you dispense with your leisure, I would by and by have
    some speech with you ; the satisfaction I would require is likewise
    your own benefit.
ISAB. I have no superfluous leisure ; my stay must be stolen out of
    other affairs   but I will attend you awhile.   [*walks apart.*
DUKE. Son, I have overheard what hath pass'd between you and your
    sister.   Angelo had never the purpose to corrupt her ; only he
    hath made an assay of her virtue to practise his judgment with the
    disposition of natures.   She, having the truth of honour in her,
    hath made him that gracious denial which he is most glad to
    receive.   I am confessor to Angelo, and I know this to be true ;
    therefore prepare yourself to death.   Do not satisfy your resolu-
    tion with hopes that are fallible ; to-morrow you must die ; go to
    your knees and make ready.   169
CLAUD. Let me ask my sister pardon.   I am so out of love with life
    that I will sue to be rid of it.
DUKE. Hold you there.   Farewell. [*exit* CLAUDIO.] Provost, a word
    with you.

Re-enter PROVOST.

PRO. What's your will, father ?   174
DUKE. That, now you are come, you will be gone.   Leave me a while
    with the maid ; my mind promises with my habit no loss shall
    touch her by my company.
PROV. In good time.   [*exit* PROVOST.
DUKE. The hand that hath made you fair hath made you good ; the
    goodness that is cheap in beauty makes beauty brief in goodness ;
    but grace, being the soul of your complexion, shall keep the body
    of it ever fair.   The assault that Angelo hath made to you,
    fortune hath convey'd to my understanding : and, but that
    frailty hath examples for his falling, I should wonder at Angelo.
    How will you do to content this substitute, and to save your
    brother ?   186
ISAB. I am now going to resolve him ; I had rather my brother die
    by the law than my son should be unlawfully born.   But, O, how
    much is the good Duke deceiv'd in Angelo ! If ever he return,
    and I can speak to him, I will open my lips in vain, or discover his
    government.   191
DUKE. That shall not be much amiss ; yet, as the matter now stands,
    he will avoid your accusation : he made trial of you only.   There-
    fore fasten your ear on my advisings ; to the love I have in doing
    good a remedy presents itself.   I do make myself believe that
    you may most uprighteously do a poor wronged lady a merited
    benefit ; redeem your brother from the angry law ; do no stain
    to your own gracious person : and much please the absent Duke,
    if peradventure he shall ever return to have hearing of this business.
ISAB. Let me hear you speak farther ; I have spirit to do anything
    that appears not foul in the truth of my spirit.   202
DUKE. Virtue is bold, and goodness never fearful.   Have you not

SCENE 13
*Interior. The Prison.
Outside Claudio's Cell.
Night.*
DUKE, ISABELLA,
CLAUDIO

CLAUDIO *remains.*
'Provost a word with
you' omitted.

Lines 174–178
omitted.

SCENE 14
*Interior. The Prison.
The Provost's Room.
Night.*
DUKE, ISABELLA

heard speak of Mariana, the sister of Frederick, the great soldier
who miscarried at sea ?

ISAB. I have heard of the lady, and good words went with her name.

DUKE. She should this Angelo have married ; was affianced to her
by oath, and the nuptial appointed ; between which time of the
contract and limit of the solemnity her brother Frederick
was wreck'd at sea, having in that perished vessel the dowry of
his sister.   But mark how heavily this befell to the poor gentlewoman : there she lost a noble and renowned brother, in his
love toward her ever most kind and natural ; with him the
portion and sinew of her fortune, her marriage-dowry ; with
both, her combinate husband, this well-seeming Angelo.   217

ISAB. Can this be so ? Did Angelo so leave her ?

DUKE. Left her in her tears, and dried not one of them with his
comfort ; swallowed his vows whole, pretending in her discoveries
of dishonour , in few, bestow'd her on her own lamentation,
which she yet wears for his sake ; and he, a marble to her tears,
is washed with them, but relents not.   223

ISAB. What a merit were it in death to take this poor maid from the
world ! What corruption in this life that it will let this man live !
But how out of this can she avail ?

DUKE. It is a rupture that you may easily heal ; and the cure of it not
only saves your brother, but keeps you from dishonour in doing it.

ISAB. Show me how, good father.   230

DUKE. This forenamed maid hath yet in her the continuance of her
first affection ; his unjust unkindness, that in all reason should
have quenched her love, hath, like an impediment in the current,
made it more violent and unruly.   Go you to Angelo ; answer
his requiring with a plausible obedience ; agree with his demands
to the point ; only refer yourself to this advantage : first, that
your stay with him may not be long ; that the time may have all
shadow and silence in it ; and the place answer to convenience.
This being granted in course—and now follows all : we shall
advise this wronged maid to stead up your appointment, go in
your place.   If the encounter acknowledge itself hereafter, it
may compel him to her recompense ; and here, by this, is your
brother saved, your honour untainted, the poor Mariana advan-
taged, and the corrupt deputy scaled.   The maid will I frame and
make fit for his attempt.   If you think well to carry this as you
may, the doubleness of the benefit defends the deceit from reproof.
What think you of it ?

ISAB. The image of it gives me content already ; and I trust it will
grow to a most prosperous perfection.   251

DUKE. It lies much in your holding up.   Haste you speedily to
Angelo ; if for this night he entreat you to his bed, give him
promise of satisfaction.   I will presently to Saint Luke's ; there,
at the moated grange, resides this dejected Mariana.   At that
place call upon me ; and dispatch with Angelo, that it may be
quickly.   257

ISAB. I thank you for this comfort.   Fare you well, good father.

                                          [*exeunt severally.*

SCENE II. *The street before the prison.*

Enter, on one side, DUKE *disguised as before ; on the other,* ELBOW, *and* OFFICERS *with* POMPEY.

ELB. Nay, if there be no remedy for it, but tha: you will needs buy and sell men and women like beasts, we shall have all the world drink brown and white bastard.

DUKE. O heavens ! what stuff is here ? 4

POM. 'Twas never merry world since, of two usuries, the merriest was put down, and the worser allow'd by order of law a furr'd gown to keep him warm ; and furr'd with fox on lamb-skins too, to signify that craft, being richer than innocency, stands for the facing.

ELB. Come your way, sir. Bless you, good father friar. 10

DUKE. And you, good brother father. What offence hath this man made you, sir ?

FLB. Marry, sir, he hath offended the law ; and, sir, we take him to be a thief too, sir, for we have found upon him, sir, a strange picklock, which we have sent to the deputy. 15

DUKE. Fie, sirrah, a bawd, a wicked bawd !
The evil that thou causest to be done,
That is thy means to live. Do thou but think
What 'tis to cram a maw or clothe a back
From such a filthy vice ; say to thyself 20
' From their abominable and beastly touches
I drink, I eat, array myself, and live '.
Canst thou believe thy living is a life,
So stinkingly depending ? Go mend, go mend.

POM. Indeed, it does stink in some sort, sir ; but yet, sir, I would prove— 26

DUKE. Nay, if the devil have given thee proofs for sin,
Thou wilt prove his. Take him to prison, officer ;
Correction and instruction must both work
Ere this rude beast will profit. 30

ELB. He must before the deputy, sir ; he has given him warning. The deputy cannot abide a whoremaster ; if he be a whore-monger, and comes before him, he were as good go a mile on his errand.

DUKE. That we were all, as some would seem to be, 35
From our faults, as his faults from seeming, free.

ELB. His neck will come to your waist—a cord, sir.

Enter LUCIO.

POM. I spy comfort ; I cry bail. Here's a gentleman, and a friend of mine. 39

LUCIO. How now, noble Pompey ! What, at the wheels of Cæsar ? Art thou led in triumph ? What, is there none of Pygmalion's images, newly made woman, to be had now for putting the hand in the pocket and extracting it clutch'd ? What reply, ha ? What say'st thou to this tune, matter, and method ? Is't not drown'd i' th' last rain, ha ? What say'st thou, trot ? Is the world as it was, man ? Which is the way ? Is it sad, and few words ? or how ? The trick of it ? 48

DUKE. Still thus, and thus ; still worse !

SCENE 15
Exterior. A Street outside the Prison. Night.

Lines 35-36 omitted.

'What reply, ha? . . . last rain, ha' omitted.

LUCIO. How doth my dear morsel, thy mistress ? Procures she still, ha ?

POM. Troth, sir, she hath eaten up all her beef, and she is herself in the tub.

LUCIO. Why, 'tis good ; it is the right of it ; it must be so ; ever your fresh whore and your powder'd bawd—an unshunn'd consequence ; it must be so.   Art going to prison, Pompey ?   57

POM. Yes, faith, sir.

LUCIO. Why, 'tis not amiss, Pompey, Farewell ; go, say I sent thee thither.   For debt, Pompey—or how ?

ELB. For being a bawd, for being a bawd.   61

LUCIO. Well, then, imprison him.   If imprisonment be the due of a bawd, why, 'tis his right.   Bawd is he doubtless, and of antiquity, too ; bawd-born.   Farewell, good Pompey.   Commend me to the prison, Pompey.   You will turn good husband now, Pompey ; you will keep the house.   66

POM. I hope, sir, your good worship will be my bail.

LUCIO. No, indeed, will I not, Pompey ; it is not the wear.   I will pray, Pompey, to increase your bondage.   If you take it not patiently, why, your mettle is the more.   Adieu, trusty Pompey. Bless you, friar.   71

DUKE. And you.

LUCIO. Does Bridget paint still, Pompey, ha ?

ELB. Come your ways, sir ; come.

POM. You will not bail me then, sir ?   75

LUCIO. Then, Pompey, nor now.   What news abroad, friar ? what news ?

ELB. Come your ways, sir ; come.

LUCIO. Go to kennel, Pompey, go.
                    [*exeunt* ELBOW, POMPEY *and* OFFICERS.
What news, friar, of the Duke ?   80

DUKE. I know none.   Can you tell me of any ?

LUCIO. Some say he is with the Emperor of Russia ; other some, he is in Rome ; but where is he, think you ?

DUKE. I know not where ; but wheresoever, I wish him well.   85

LUCIO. It was a mad fantastical trick of him to steal from the state and usurp the beggary he was never born to.   Lord Angelo dukes it well in his absence ; he puts transgression to't.

DUKE. He does well in't.   90

LUCIO. A little more lenity to lechery would do no harm in him. Something too crabbed that way, friar.

DUKE. It is too general a vice, and severity must cure it.

LUCIO. Yes, in good sooth, the vice is of a great kindred ; it is well allied ; but it is impossible to extirp it quite, friar, till eating and drinking be put down.   They say this Angelo was not made by man and woman after this downright way of creation.   Is it true, think you ?   98

DUKE. How should he be made, then ?

LUCIO. Some report a sea-maid spawn'd him ; some, that he was begot between two stock-fishes.   But it is certain that when he makes water his urine is congeal'd ice ; that I know to be true. And he is a motion generative ; that's infallible.

DUKE. You are pleasant, sir, and speak apace.   105

LUCIO. Why, what a ruthless thing is this in him, for the rebellion of

SCENE 16
Exterior. Outside the Prison. Night.
LUCIO, POMPEY, DUKE, ELBOW

a codpiece to take away the life of a man . Would the Duke that
is absent have done this ? Ere he would have hang'd a man for
the getting a hundred bastards, he would have paid for the nursing
a thousand.   He had some feeling of the sport ; he knew the
service, and that instructed him to mercy.   112
DUKE. I never heard the absent Duke much detected for women ; he
was not inclin'd that way.
LUCIO. O, sir, you are deceiv'd.
DUKE. 'Tis not possible.
LUCIO. Who—not the Duke ? Yes, your beggar of fifty ; and his
use was to put a ducat in her clack-dish.   The Duke had crotchets
in him. He would be drunk too ; that .et me inform you.   120
DUKE. You do him wrong, surely.
LUCIO. Sir, I was an inward of his. A shy fellow was the Duke ;
and I believe I know the cause of his withdrawing.
DUKE. What, I prithee, might be the cause ?   125
LUCIO. No, pardon ; 'tis a secret must be lock'd within the teeth and
the lips ; but this I can let you understand : the greater file of
the subject held the Duke to be wise.
DUKE. Wise ? Why, no question but he was.
LUCIO. A very superficial, ignorant, unweighing fellow.   130
DUKE. Either this is envy in you, folly, or mistaking ; the very stream of
his life, and the business he hath helmed, must, upon a warranted
need, give him a better proclamation.   Let him be but testimonied
in his own bringings-forth, and he shall appear to the envious a
scholar, a statesman, and a soldier.   Therefore you speak
unskilfully ;   or, if your knowledge be more, it is much dark'ned
in your malice.
LUCIO. Sir, I know him, and I love him.   139
DUKE. Love talks with better knowledge, and knowledge with dearer
love.
LUCIO. Come, sir, I know what I know.
DUKE. I can hardly believe that, since you know not what you speak.
But, if ever the Duke return, as our prayers are he may, let me
desire you to make your answer before him. If it be honest you
have spoke, you have courage to maintain it ; I am bound to call
upon you ; and I pray you your name ?
LUCIO. Sir, my name is Lucio, well known to the Duke.   150
DUKE. He shall know you better, sir, if I may live to report you.
LUCIO. I fear you not.
DUKE. O, you hope the Duke will return no more ; or you imagine me
too unhurtful an opposite. But, indeed, I can do you little
harm : you'll forswear this again.   156
LUCIO. I'll be hang'd first. Thou art deceiv'd in me, friar. But no
more of this. Canst thou tell if Claudio die to-morrow or no ?
DUKE. Why should he die, sir ?   160
LUCIO. Why ? For filling a bottle with a tun-dish. I would the
Duke we talk of were return'd again. This ungenitur'd agent
will unpeople the province with continency ; sparrows must not
build in his house-eaves because they are lecherous. The Duke
yet would have dark deeds darkly answered ; he would never
bring them to light. Would he were return'd ! Marry, this Claudio
is condemned for untrussing. Farewell, good friar ; I prithee
pray for me. The Duke, I say to thee again, would eat mutton

on Fridays. He's not past it yet ; and, I say to thee, he would
mouth with a beggar though she smelt brown bread and garlic.
Say that I said so. Farewell.   [*exit.*
DUKE. No might nor greatness in mortality
Can censure scape ; back-wounding calumny
The whitest virtue strikes. What king so strong   175
Can tie the gall up in the slanderous tongue ?
But who comes here ?

Enter ESCALUS, PROVOST, *and* OFFICERS *with* MISTRESS OVERDONE.

ESCAL. Go, away with her to prison.
MRS. OV. Good my lord, be good to me ; your honour is accounted
a merciful man ; good my lord.   180
ESCAL. Double and treble admonition, and still forfeit in the same
kind ! This would make mercy swear and play the tyrant.
PROV. A bawd of eleven years' continuance, may it please your
honour.   185
MRS. OV. My Lord, this is one Lucio's information against me.
Mistress Kate Keepdown was with child by him in the Duke's
time ; he promis'd her marriage. His child is a year and a
quarter old come Philip and Jacob ; I have kept it myself ; and
see how he goes about to abuse me.   191
ESCAL. That fellow is a fellow of much licence. Let him be call'd
before us. Away with her to prison. Go to ; no more words.

[*exeunt* OFFICERS *with* MISTRESS OVERDONE.

Provost, my brother Angelo will not be alter'd : Claudio must die
to-morrow. Let him be furnish'd with divines, and have all
charitable preparation. If my brother wrought by my pity, it
should not be so with him.
PROV. So please you, this friar hath been with him, and advis'd him
for th' entertainment of death.   200
ESCAL. Good even, good father.
DUKE. Bliss and goodness on you !
ESCAL. Of whence are you ?
DUKE. Not of this country, though my chance is now
To use it for my time. I am a brother   205
Of gracious order, late come from the See
In special business from his Holiness.
ESCAL. What news abroad i' th' world ?
DUKE. None, but that there is so great a fever on goodness that the
dissolution of it must cure it. Novelty is only in request ; and,
as it is, as dangerous to be aged in any kind of course as it is
virtuous to be constant in any undertaking. There is scarce
truth enough alive to make societies secure ; but security enough
to make fellowships accurst. Much upon this riddle runs the
wisdom of the world. This news is old enough, yet it is every
day's news. I pray you, sir, of what disposition was the Duke ?
ESCAL. One that, above all other strifes, contended especially to know
himself.
DUKE. What pleasure was he given to ?   220
ESCAL. Rather rejoicing to see another merry than merry at anything
which profess'd to make him rejoice ; a gentleman of all temper-
ance. But leave we him to his events, with a prayer they may
prove prosperous ; and let me desire to know how you find

| Line 177 omitted.

SCENE 17
Interior. The Brothel.
Night.

61

Claudio prepar'd. I am made to understand that you have lent
him visitation.   226
DUKE. He professes to have received no sinister measure from his
judge, but most willingly humbles himself to the determination of
justice.   Yet had he framed to himself, by the instruction of his
frailty, many deceiving promises of life ; which I, by my good
leisure, have discredited to him, and now he is resolv'd to die.   232
ESCAL. You have paid the heavens your function, and the prisoner
the very debt of your calling.   I have labour'd for the poor
gentleman to the extremest shore of my modesty ; but my
brother justice have I found so severe that he hath forc'd me to
tell him he is indeed Justice.
DUKE. If his own life answer the straitness of his proceeding, it shall
become him well ; wherein if he chance to fail, he hath sentenc'd
himself.   240
ESCAL. I am going to visit the prisoner.   Fare you well.
DUKE. Peace be with you !   [exeunt ESCALUS AND PROVOST.

> He who the sword of heaven will bear
> Should be as holy as severe ;
> Pattern in himself to know,   245
> Grace to stand, and virtue go :
> More nor less to others paying
> Than by self-offences weighing.
> Shame to him whose cruel striking
> Kills for faults of his own liking !   250
> Twice treble shame on Angelo,
> To weed my vice and let his grow !
> O, what may man within him hide,
> Though angel on the outward side !
> How may likeness, made in crimes,   255
> Make a practice on the times,
> To draw with idle spiders' strings
> Most ponderous and substantial things !
> Craft against vice I must apply.
> With Angelo to-night shall lie
> His old betrothed but despised ;   260
> So disguise shall, by th' disguised,
> Pay with falsehood false exacting,
> And perform an old contracting.   [exit.

ACT FOUR

SCENE I. *The moated grange at Saint Luke's.*
Enter MARIANA ; *and* BOY *singing.*
Song.

SCENE 18
*Exterior. A Summer
House in Mariana's
Garden. Night.*

Take, O, take those lips away,
    That so sweetly were forsworn ;
And those eyes, the break of day,
    Lights that do mislead the morn ;
But my kisses bring again, bring again ;   5
Seals of love, but seal'd in vain, seal'd in vain.

Enter DUKE, *disguised as before.*

MARI. Break off thy song, and haste thee quick away ;　　　Lines 7–9 omitted.
　　Here comes a man of comfort, whose advice
　　Hath often still'd my brawling discontent.　　　[exit BOY.　BOY remains.
　I cry you mercy, sir, and well could wish　　　　　　10
　　You had not found me here so musical.
　　Let me excuse me, and believe me so,
　　My mirth it much displeas'd, but pleas'd my woe.
DUKE. 'Tis good ; though music oft hath such a charm
　　To make bad good and good provoke to harm.　　　15
　　I pray you tell me hath anybody inquir'd for me here to-day.
　　Much upon this time have I promis'd here to meet.
MARI. You have not been inquir'd after ; I have sat here all day.

　　　　　　　　Enter ISABELLA.　　　　　　　ISABELLA enters later.

DUKE. I do constantly believe you.　The time is come even now.　I
　　shall crave your forbearance a little.　May be I will call upon
　　you anon, for some advantage to yourself.
MARI. I am always bound to you.　　　　　　　[exit.　MARIANA remains.
DUKE. Very well met, and well come.　　　　　　　　　ISABELLA enters.
　　What is the news from this good deputy ?　　　　25
ISAB. He hath a garden circummur'd with brick,
　　Whose western side is with a vineyard back'd ;
　　And to that vineyard is a planched gate
　　That makes his opening with this bigger key.
　　This other doth command a little door　　　　　　30
　　Which from the vineyard to the garden leads.
　　There have I made my promise
　　Upon the heavy middle of the night
　　To call upon him.
DUKE. But shall you on your knowledge find this way ?　　　35
ISAB. I have ta'en a due and wary note upon't ;
　　With whispering and most guilty diligence,
　　In action all of precept, he did show me
　　The way twice o'er.
DUKE.　　　　　　　　Are there no other tokens
　　Between you 'greed concerning her observance ?　　　40
ISAB. No, none, but only a repair i' th' dark ;
　　And that I have possess'd him my most stay
　　Can be but brief ; for I have made him know
　　I have a servant comes with me along,
　　That stays upon me ; whose persuasion is　　　　45
　　I come about my brother.
DUKE.　　　　　　　　'Tis well borne up.
　　I have not yet made known to Mariana
　　A word of this.　What ho, within ! come forth.　　　'What ho, within!
　　　　　　　　　　　　　　　　　　　　　　　　　come forth' and stage
　　　　　　　Re-enter MARIANA.　　　　　　　　direction omitted.
　I pray you be acquainted with this maid ;
　　She comes to do you good.
ISAB.　　　　　　　I do desire the like.　　　　　50
DUKE. Do you persuade yourself that I respect you ?
MARI. Good friar, I know you do, and have found it.
DUKE. Take, then, this your companion by the hand,
　　Who hath a story ready for your ear.

I shall attend your leisure ; but make haste ;   55
The vaporous night approaches.
MARI. Will't please you walk aside ?
                              [*exeunt* MARIANA *and* ISABELLA.
DUKE. O place and greatness ! Millions of false eyes
Are stuck upon thee. Volumes of report
Run with these false, and most contrarious quest   60
Upon thy doings. Thousand escapes of wit
Make thee the father of their idle dream,
And rack thee in their fancies.

Re-enter MARIANA *and* ISABELLA.

                              Welcome, how agreed ?
ISAB. She'll take the enterprise upon her, father,
If you advise it.
DUKE.   It is not my consent,   65
But my entreaty too.
ISAB.   Little have you to say,
When you depart from him, but, soft and low,
'Remember now my brother '.
MARI.   Fear me not.
DUKE. Nor, gentle daughter, fear you not at all.
He is your husband on a pre-contract.   70
To bring you thus together 'tis no sin,
Sith that the justice of your title to him
Doth flourish the deceit. Come, let us go ;
Our corn's to reap, for yet our tithe's to sow.   [*exeunt.*

SCENE II. *The prison.*

Enter PROVOST *and* POMPEY.

PROV. Come hither, sirrah. Can you cut off a man's head ?
POM. If the man be a bachelor, sir, I can ; but if he be a married
man, he's his wife's head, and I can never cut off a woman's
head.   4
PROV. Come, sir, leave me your snatches and yield me a direct
answer. To-morrow morning are to die Claudio and Barnardine.
Here is in our prison a common executioner, who in his office
lacks a helper ; if you will take it on you to assist him, it shall
redeem you from your gyves ; if not, you shall have your full time
of imprisonment, and your deliverance with an unpitied whipping,
for you have been a notorious bawd.   12
POM. Sir, I have been an unlawful bawd time out of mind ; but yet
I will be content to be a lawful hangman. I would be glad to
receive some instructions from my fellow partner.
PROV. What ho, Abhorson ! Where's Abhorson there ?

Enter ABHORSON.

ABHOR. Do you call, sir ?   18
PROV. Sirrah, here's a fellow will help you to-morrow in your execution. If you think it meet, compound with him by the year, and
let him abide here with you ; if not, use him for the present, and
dismiss him. He cannot plead his estimation with you ; he hath
been a bawd.   23

SCENE 19
Interior. The Prison.
Pompey's Cell. Night.

SCENE 20
Interior. The Prison.
Abhorson's Room.
Night.
ABHORSON, PROVOST,
POMPEY

Kenneth Colley as the Duke

Angelo (Tim Pigott-Smith) and Isabella (Kate Nelligan)

Christopher Strauli as Claudio and
Yolande Palfrey as Juliet

Left to right: Angelo (Tim Pigott-Smith), Escalus (Kevin Stoney), The Duke
(Kenneth Colley), and Mariana (Jacqueline Pearce)

ABHOR. A bawd, sir? Fie upon him! He will discredit our mystery.
PROV. Go to, sir; you weigh equally; a feather will turn the scale.

                                                       [exit. | PROVOST *remains.*
POM. Pray, sir, by your good favour—for surely, sir, a good favour
    you have but that you have a hanging look—do you call, sir, your
    occupation a mystery?   30
ABHOR. Ay, sir; a mystery.
POM. Painting, sir, I have heard say, is a mystery; and your whores,
    sir, being members of my occupation, using painting, do prove
    my occupation a mystery; but what mystery there should be in
    hanging, if I should be hang'd, I cannot imagine.   36
ABHOR. Sir, it is a mystery.
POM. Proof?
ABHOR. Every true man's apparel fits your thief: if it be too little for
    your thief, your true man thinks it big enough; if it be too big
    for your thief, your thief thinks it little enough; so every true
    man's apparel fits your thief.   42

                Re-enter PROVOST. | Stage direction
PROV. Are you agreed?   omitted.
POM. Sir, I will serve him; for I do find your hangman is a more
    penitent trade than your bawd; he doth oftener ask forgiveness.
PROV. You, sirrah, provide your block and your axe to-morrow four
    o'clock.   48
ABHOR. Come on, bawd; I will instruct thee in my trade; follow.
POM. I do desire to learn, sir; and I hope, if you have occasion to
    use me for your own turn, you shall find me yare; for truly, sir,
    for your kindness I owe you a good turn.   54 | Lines 55–57 omitted.
PROV. Call hither Barnardine and Claudio.
               [exeunt ABHORSON *and* POMPEY.
Th' one has my pity; not a jot the other,
Being a murderer, though he were my brother.

                Enter CLAUDIO.

Look, here's the warrant, Claudio, for thy death;   SCENE 21
'Tis now dead midnight, and by eight to-morrow   *Interior. The Prison.*
Thou must be made immortal. Where's Barnardine? 60   *Outside Claudio's Cell.*
CLAUD. As fast lock'd up in sleep as guiltless labour   *Night.*
    When it lies starkly in the traveller's bones.   PROVOST, CLAUDIO
    He will not wake.
PROV.   Who can do good on him?
    Well, go, prepare yourself. [*knocking within.*] But hark, what
    noise?
Heaven give your spirits comfort!   [*exit* CLAUDIO.
              [*knocking continues.*] By and by. 65   SCENE 22
I hope it is some pardon or reprieve   *Interior. The Prison.*
For the most gentle Claudio.   *The Provost's Room.*
                                    Night.
       Enter DUKE, *disguised as before.*   PROVOST, DUKE
           Welcome, father.
DUKE. The best and wholesom'st spirits of the night
    Envelop you, good Provost! Who call'd here of late?
PROV. None, since the curfew rung.   70
DUKE. Not Isabel?

PROV. No.
DUKE. They will then, ere't be long.
PROV. What comfort is for Claudio ?
DUKE. There's some in hope.
PROV. It is a bitter deputy.
DUKE. Not so, not so ; his life is parallel'd   75
Even with the stroke and line of his great justice ;
He doth with holy abstinence subdue
That in himself which he spurs on his pow'r
To qualify in others.   Were he meal'd with that
Which he corrects, then were he tyrannous ;   80
But this being so, he's just. [*knocking within.*] Now are they come. | Lines 81, from
                                        [*exit* PROVOST. | '[knocking within]', to
This is a gentle provost ; seldom when | 87 omitted.
The steeled gaoler is the friend of men.   [*knocking within.*]
How now, what noise ! That spirit's possess'd with haste | Lines 84–85 see below.
That wounds th' unsisting postern with these strokes.   85

                Re-enter PROVOST.

PROV. There he must stay until the officer
Arise to let him in ; he is call'd up.
DUKE. Have you no countermand for Claudio yet
But he must die to-morrow ?
PROV.   None, sir, none.
DUKE. As near the dawning, Provost, as it is,   90
You shall hear more ere morning.
PROV.   Happily
You something know ; yet I believe there comes
No countermand ; no such example have we.
Besides, upon the very siege of justice,
Lord Angelo hath to the public ear   95
Profess'd the contrary.   *The entrance bell

         Enter a MESSENGER.   *rings.* Lines 84–85,
                                      'How now . . . these
           This is his lordship's man.   *strokes', spoken by*
DUKE. And here comes Claudio's pardon.   DUKE *in line 96.*
MESS. My lord hath sent you this note ; and by me this further charge,
that you swerve not from the smallest article of it, neither in
time, matter, or other circumstance. Good morrow ; for as I
take it, it is almost day.   101
PROV. I shall obey him.   [*exit* MESSENGER.
DUKE. [*aside.*] This is his pardon, purchas'd by such sin
For which the pardoner himself is in ;
Hence hath offence his quick celerity,   105
When it is borne in high authority.
When vice makes mercy, mercy's so extended
That for the fault's love is th' offender friended.
Now, sir, what news ?   109
PROV. I told you : Lord Angelo, belike thinking me remiss in mine
office, awakens me with this unwonted putting-on ; methinks
strangely, for he hath not us'd it before.
DUKE. Pray you, let's hear.   113
PROV. [*reads*] ' Whatsoever you may hear to the contrary, let Claudio
be executed by four of the clock, and, in the afternoon, Barnardine.

For my better satisfaction, let me have Claudio's head sent me
by five. Let this be duly performed, with a thought that more
depends on it than we must yet deliver. Thus fail not to do
your office, as you will answer it at your peril.'
What say you to this, sir ?   120
DUKE. What is that Barnardine who is to be executed in th' afternoon ?
PROV. A Bohemian born ; but here nurs'd up and bred. One that
is a prisoner nine years old.
DUKE. How came it that the absent Duke had not either deliver'd him
to his liberty or executed him ? I have heard it was ever his
manner to do so.
PROV. His friends still wrought reprieves for him ; and, indeed, his
fact, till now in the government of Lord Angelo, came not to an
undoubted proof.   130
DUKE. It is now apparent ?
PROV. Most manifest, and not denied by himself.   *They walk to*
DUKE. Hath he borne himself penitently in prison ? How seems he   *Barnardine's cell.*
to be touch'd ?   134
PROV. A man that apprehends death no more dreadfully but as a
drunken sleep ; careless, reckless, and fearless, of what's past,
present, or to come ; insensible of mortality and desperately
mortal.   138
DUKE. He wants advice.
PROV. He will hear none. He hath evermore had the liberty of the
prison ; give him leave to escape hence, he would not ; drunk
many times a day, if not many days entirely drunk. We have
very oft awak'd him, as if to carry him to execution, and show'd
him a seeming warrant for it ; it hath not moved him at all.   145
DUKE. More of him anon. There is written in your brow, Provost,
honesty and constancy. If I read it not truly, my ancient skill
beguiles me ; but in the boldness of my cunning I will lay myself
in hazard. Claudio, whom here you have warrant to execute, is
no greater forfeit to the law than Angelo who hath sentenc'd
him. To make you understand this in a manifested effect, I
crave but four days' respite ; for the which you are to do me
both a present and a dangerous courtesy.
PROV. Pray, sir, in what ?   155
DUKE. In the delaying death.
PROV. Alack ! How may I do it, having the hour limited, and an   *They return to the*
express command, under penalty, to deliver his head in the view   *Provost's office.*
of Angelo ? I may make my case as Claudio's, to cross this in the
smallest.   160
DUKE. By the vow of mine order, I warrant you, if my instructions
may be your guide. Let this Barnardine be this morning
executed, and his head borne to Angelo.
PROV. Angelo hath seen them both, and will discover the favour. 165
DUKE. O, death's a great disguiser ; and you may add to it. Shave
the head and tie the beard ; and say it was the desire of the
penitent to be so bar'd before his death. You know the course
is common. If anything fall to you upon this more than thanks
and good fortune, by the saint whom I profess, I will plead
against it with my life.   171
PROV. Pardon me, good father ; it is against my oath.
DUKE. Were you sworn to the Duke, or to the deputy ?

PROV. To him and to his substitutes.

DUKE. You will think you have made no offence if the Duke avouch
the justice of your dealing ? 176

PROV. But what likelihood is in that ?

DUKE. Not a resemblance, but a certainty. Yet since I see you fearful,
that neither my coat, integrity, nor persuasion, can with ease
attempt you, I will go further than I meant, to pluck all fears out
of you. Look you, sir, here is the hand and seal of the Duke.
You know the character, I doubt not ; and the signet is not strange
to you.

PROV. I know them both. 184

DUKE. The contents of this is the return of the Duke ; you shall
anon over-read it at your pleasure, where you shall find within
these two days he will be here. This is a thing that Angelo
knows not ; for he this very day receives letters of strange tenour,
perchance of the Duke's death, perchance entering into some
monastery ; but, by chance, nothing of what is writ. Look,
th' unfolding star calls up the shepherd. Put not yourself into
amazement how these things should be : all difficulties are but
easy when they are known. Call your executioner, and off with
Barnardine's head. I will give him a present shrift, and advise
him for a better place. Yet you are amaz'd, but this shall
absolutely resolve you. Come away ; it is almost clear dawn.

[exeunt.

SCENE III. The prison.

Enter POMPEY.

SCENE 23
Interior. The Prison.
A Corridor. Day

POM. I am as well acquainted here as I was in our house of profession ;
one would think it were Mistress Overdone's own house, for here
be many of her old customers. First, here's young Master
Rash ; he's in for a commodity of brown paper and old ginger,
nine score and seventeen pounds, of which he made five marks
ready money. Marry, then ginger was not much in request, for
the old women were all dead. Then is there here one Master
Caper, at the suit of Master Threepile the mercer, for some four
suits of peach-colour'd satin, which now peaches him a beggar.
Then have we here young Dizy, and young Master Deepvow,
and Master Copperspur, and Master Starvelackey, the rapier and
dagger man, and young Dropheir that kill'd lusty Pudding, and
Master Forthlight the tilter, and brave Master Shootie the great
traveller, and wild Halfcan that stabb'd Pots, and, I think, forty
more—all great doers in our trade, and are now ' for the Lord's
sake '. 18

Enter ABHORSON.

ABHOR. Sirrah, bring Barnardine hither.

POM. Master Barnardine ! You must rise and be hang'd, Master
Barnardine !

ABHOR. What ho, Barnardine !

BARNAR. [Within] A pox o' your throats ! Who makes that noise
there ? What are you ?

POM. Your friends, sir ; the hangman. You must be so good, sir,
to rise and be put to death. 26

SCENE 24
Interior. The Prison.
Outside Barnardine's
Cell. Day.
POMPEY, ABHORSON,
BARNARDINE

BARNAR. [*Within*]   Away, you rogue, away : I am sleepy.
ABHOR. Tell him he must awake, and that quickly too.
POM. Pray, Master Barnardine, awake till you are executed, and sleep
    afterwards.   30
ABHOR. Go in to him, and fetch him out.
POM. He is coming, sir, he is coming ; I hear his straw rustle.

Enter BARNARDINE.

ABHOR. Is the axe upon the block, sirrah ?
POM. Very ready, sir.   35
BARNAR. How now, Abhorson, what's the news with you ?
ABHOR. Truly, sir, I would desire you to clap into your prayers ; for,
    look you, the warrant's come.
BARNAR. You rogue, I have been drinking all night ; I am not fitted
    for't.   40
POM. O, the better, sir ! For he that drinks all night and is hanged
    betimes in the morning may sleep the sounder all the next day.

Enter DUKE, *disguised as before.*

ABHOR. Look you, sir, here comes your ghostly father. Do we jest
    now, think you ?   45
DUKE. Sir, induced by my charity, and hearing how hastily you are
    to depart, I am come to advise you, comfort you, and pray with
    you.
BARNAR. Friar, not I ; I have been drinking hard all night, and I will
    have more time to prepare me, or they shall beat out my brains
    with billets. I will not consent to die this day, that's certain.   52
DUKE. O, sir, you must ; and therefore I beseech you
    Look forward on the journey you shall go.
BARNAR. I swear I will not die to-day for any man's persuasion.
DUKE. But hear you—
BARNAR. Not a word ; if you have anything to say to me, come to
    my ward ; for thence will not I to-day.   [*exit.*
DUKE. Unfit to live or die. O gravel heart !   60 | Lines 60–61 omitted.
    After him, fellows ; bring him to the block.

    [*exeunt* ABHORSON *and* POMPEY.

Enter PROVOST.

PROV. Now, sir, how do you find the prisoner.
DUKE. A creature unprepar'd, unmeet for death ;
    And to transport him in the mind he is
    Were damnable.
PROV.   Here in the prison, father,   65
    There died this morning of a cruel fever
    One Ragozine, a most notorious pirate,
    A man of Claudio's years , his beard and head
    Just of his colour   What if we do omit
    This reprobate till he were well inclin'd,   70
    And satisfy the deputy with the visage
    Of Ragozine, more like to Claudio ?
DUKE. O, 'tis an accident that heaven provides !
    Dispatch it presently ; the hour draws on
    Prefix'd by Angelo. See this be done,   75
    And sent according to command ; whiles I

Persuade this rude wretch willingly to die.
PROV. This shall be done, good father, presently.
But Barnardine must die this afternoon ;   *They walk to the*
And how shall we continue Claudio,   80   *Provost's room.*
To save me from the danger that might come
If he were known alive ?
DUKE.   Let this be done :
Put them in secret holds, both Barnardine and Claudio.
Ere twice the sun hath made his journal greeting
To the under generation, you shall find   85
Your safety manifested.
PPOV. I am your free dependant.
DUKE. Quick, dispatch, and send the head to Angelo. [*exit* PROVOST.
Now will I write letters to Angelo—
The Provost, he shall bear them—whose contents   90
Shall witness to him I am near at home,
And that, by great injunctions, I am bound
To enter publicly.   Him I'll desire
To meet me at the consecrated fount,
A league below the city ; and from thence,   95
By cold gradation and well-balanc'd form,
We shall proceed with Angelo.

Re-enter PROVOST.

PROV. Here is the head ; I'll carry it myself.
DUKE. Convenient is it.   Make a swift return ;
For I would commune with you of such things   100
That want no ear but yours.
PROV.   I'll make all speed.   [*exit*
ISAB. [*within*] Peace, ho, be here !
DUKE. The tongue of Isabel.   She's come to know
If yet her brother's pardon be come hither ;
But I will keep her ignorant of her good,   10
To make her heavenly comforts of despair
When it is least expected.

Enter ISABELLA.

ISAB.   Ho, by your leave !
DUKE. Good morning to you, fair and gracious daughter.
ISAB. The better, given me by so holy a man.
Hath yet the deputy sent my brother's pardon ?   110
DUKE. He hath releas'd him, Isabel, from the world.
His head is off and sent to Angelo.
ISAB. Nay, but it is not so.
DUKE.   It is no other.
Show your wisdom, daughter, in your close patience.   115
ISAB. O, I will to him and pluck out his eyes !
DUKE. You shall not be admitted to his sight.
ISAB. Unhappy Claudio ! Wretched Isabel !
Injurious world ! Most damned Angelo !
DUKE. This nor hurts him nor profits you a jot ;   120
Forbear it, therefore ; give your cause to heaven.
Mark what I say, which you shall find
By every syllable a faithful verity.

SCENE 25
*Exterior. Street outside
the Prison. Day.*
DUKE, ISABELLA
Lines 107, from 'Ho,
by your leave', to 109
omitted.

The Duke comes home to-morrow. Nay, dry your eyes.
One of our covent, and his confessor,   125
Gives me this instance. Already he hath carried
Notice to Escalus and Angelo,
Who do prepare to meet him at the gates,
There to give up their pow'r. If you can, pace your wisdom
In that good path that I would wish it go,   130
And you shall have your bosom on this wretch,
Grace of the Duke, revenges to your heart,
And general honour.
ISAB.   I am directed by you.
DUKE. This letter, then, to Friar Peter give ;   For 'Friar Peter' read
'Tis that he sent me of the Duke's return.   135   'Friar Thomas'.
Say, by this token, I desire his company
At Mariana's house to-night. Her cause and yours
I'll perfect him withal ; and he shall bring you
Before the Duke ; and to the head of Angelo
Accuse him home and home. For my poor self,   140
I am combined by a sacred vow,
And shall be absent. Wend you with this letter.
Command these fretting waters from your eyes
With a light heart ; trust not my holy order,
If I pervert your course. Who's here ?   145

Enter LUCIO.

LUCIO. Good even. Friar, where's the Provost ?
DUKE. Not within, sir.
LUCIO. O pretty Isabella, I am pale at mine heart to see thine eyes so
red. Thou must be patient. I am fain to dine and sup with
water and bran ; I dare not for my head fill my belly ; one fruitful
meal would set me to't. But they say the Duke will be here
to-morrow. By my troth, Isabel, I lov'd thy brother. If the old
fantastical Duke of dark corners had been at home, he had lived.
                                          [*exit* ISABELLA.
DUKE. Sir, the Duke is marvellous little beholding to your reports;
but the best is, he lives not in them.   156
LUCIO. Friar, thou knowest not the Duke so well as I do ; he's a
better woodman than thou tak'st him for.
DUKE. Well, you'll answer this one day. Fare ye well.
LUCIO. Nay, tarry ; I'll go along with thee ; I can tell thee pretty
tales of the Duke.   161
DUKE. You have told me too many of him already, sir, if they be
true ; if not true, none were enough.
LUCIO. I was once before him for getting a wench with child.
DUKE. Did you such a thing ?
LUCIO. Yes, marry, did I ; but I was fain to forswear it : they would
else have married me to the rotten medlar.
DUKE. Sir, your company is fairer than honest. Rest you well.   170
LUCIO. By my troth, I'll go with thee to the lane's end. If bawdy
talk offend you, we'll have very little of it. Nay, friar, I am a
kind of burr ; I shall stick.   [*exeunt*.

SCENE IV. ANGELO'S *house.*

Enter ANGELO *and* ESCALUS.

ESCAL. Every letter he hath writ hath disvouch'd other.
ANG. In most uneven and distracted manner. His actions show
　much like to madness ; pray heaven his wisdom be not tainted !
　And why meet him at the gates, and redeliver our authorities
　there ? 5
ESCAL. I guess not.
ANG. And why should we proclaim it in an hour before his ent'ring
　that, if any crave redress of injustice, they should exhibit their
　petitions in the street ?
ESCAL. He shows his reason for that : to have a dispatch of complaints;
　and to deliver us from devices hereafter, which shall then have no
　power to stand against us.
ANG. Well, I beseech you, let it be proclaim'd ;
　Betimes i' th' morn I'll call you at your house ;
　Give notice to such men of sort and suit
　As are to meet him. 15
ESCAL. I shall, sir ; fare you well.
ANG. Good night. [*exit* ESCALUS.
　This deed unshapes me quite, makes me unpregnant
　And dull to all proceedings. A deflow'red maid !
　And by an eminent body that enforc'd 20
　The law against i. ! But that her tender shame
　Will not proclaim against her maiden loss,
　How might she tongue me ! Yet reason dares her no ;
　For my authority bears a so credent bulk
　That no particular scandal once can touch 25
　But it confounds the breather. He should have liv'd,
　Save that his riotous youth, with dangerous sense,
　Might in the times to come have ta'en revenge,
　By so receiving a dishonour'd life
　With ransom of such shame. Would yet he had liv'd ! 30
　Alack, when once our grace we have forgot,
　Nothing goes right ; we would, and we would not. [*exit.*

SCENE V. *Fields without the town.*

Enter DUKE *in his own habit, and* FRIAR PETER.

DUKE. These letters at fit time deliver me. [*giving letters.*
　The Provost knows our purpose and our plot.
　The matter being afoot, keep your instruction
　And hold you ever to our special drift ;
　Though sometimes you do blench from this to that 5
　As cause doth minister. Go, call at Flavius' house,
　And tell him where I stay ; give the like notice
　To Valentinus, Rowland, and to Crassus,
　And bid them bring the trumpets to the gate ;
　But send me Flavius first.
F. PETER. It shall be speeded well. [*exit* FRIAR.

SCENE 26
*Interior. The Duke's
Audience Chamber.
Day.*

'Good night' omitted.

This scene omitted.

Enter VARRIUS.

DUKE. I thank thee, Varrius ; thou hast made good haste.   11
Come, we will walk.   There's other of our friends
Will greet us here anon. 'My gentle Varrius !   [*exeunt.*

SCENE VI. *A street near the city gate.*

Enter ISABELLA *and* MARIANA.

SCENE 27
*Exterior. A Street. Near
the City Gate. Day.*

ISAB. To speak so indirectly I am loath ;
I would say the truth ; but to accuse him so,
That is your part.   Yet I am advis'd to do it ;
He says, to veil full purpose.
MARI.   Be rul'd by him.
ISAB. Besides, he tells me that, if peradventure   5
He speak against me on the adverse side,
I should not think it strange ; for 'tis a physic
That's bitter to sweet end.
MARI. I would friar Peter—

For 'Peter' read
'Thomas'.

Enter FRIAR PETER.

Enter FRIAR THOMAS.

ISAB.   O, peace ! the friar is come.
F. PETER. Come, I have found you out a stand most fit,   10
Where you may have such vantage on the Duke
He shall not pass you. Twice have the trumpets sounded ;
The generous and gravest citizens
Have hent the gates, and very near upon
The Duke is ent'ring ; therefore, hence, away.   [*exeunt.*

Lines spoken by FRIAR
THOMAS.

ACT FIVE

SCENE I. *The city gate.*

Enter at several doors DUKE, VARRIUS, LORDS   ANGELO, ESCALUS, LUCIO,
PROVOST, OFFICERS, *and* CITIZENS.

SCENE 28
*Exterior. The City Gate.
Day.*

DUKE. My very worth cousin, fairly met !
Our old and faithful friend, we are glad to see you.
ANG. ESCAL. Happy return be to your royal Grace !
DUKE. Many and hearty thankings to you both.
We have made inquiry of you, and we hear   5
Such goodness of your justice that our soul
Cannot but yield you forth to public thanks,
Forerunning more requital.
ANG. You make my bonds still greater.
DUKE. O, your desert speaks loud ; and I should wrong it
To lock it in the wards of covert bosom,   10
When it deserves. with characters of brass,
A forted residence 'gainst the tooth of time
And razure of oblivion.   Give me your hand.
And let the subject see, to make them know
That outward courtesies would fain proclaim   15
Favours that keep within.   Come, Escalus,
You must walk by us on our other hand ,
And good supporters are you.

Enter FRIAR PETER *and* ISABELLA.
F. PETER. Now is your time ; speak loud, and kneel before him.
ISAB. Justice, O royal Duke ! Vail your regard   20
    Upon a wrong'd—I would fain have said a maid !
    O worthy Prince, dishonour not your eye
    By throwing it on any other object
    Till you have heard me in my true complaint,
    And given me justice, justice, justice, justice.   25
DUKE. Relate your wrongs. In what ? By whom ? Be brief.
    Here is Lord Angelo shall give you justice ;
    Reveal yourself to him.
ISAB.   O worthy Duke,
    You bid me seek redemption of the devil !
    Hear me yourself ; for that which I must speak   30
    Must either punish me, not being believ'd,
    Or wring redress from you. Hear me, O, hear me, here !
ANG. My lord, her wits, I fear me, are not firm ;
    She hath been a suitor to me for her brother,
    Cut off by course of justice—
ISAB.   By course of justice !   35
ANG. And she will speak most bitterly and strange.
ISAB. Most strange, but yet most truly, will I speak.
    That Angelo's forsworn, is it not strange ?
    That Angelo's a murderer, is't not strange ?
    That Angelo is an adulterous thief,   40
    An hypocrite, a virgin-violator,
    Is it not strange and strange ?
DUKE.   Nay, it is ten times strange.
ISAB. It is not truer he is Angelo
    Than this is all as true as it is strange ;
    Nay, it is ten times true ; for truth is truth   45
    To th' end of reck'ning.
DUKE.   Away with her. Poor soul,
    She speaks this in th' infirmity of sense.
ISAB. O Prince ! I conjure thee, as thou believ'st
    There is another comfort than this world,
    That thou neglect me not with that opinion   50
    That I am touch'd with madness. Make not impossible
    That which but seems unlike : 'tis not impossible
    But one, the wicked'st caitiff on the ground,
    May seem as shy, as grave, as just, as absolute,
    As Angelo ; even so may Angelo,   55
    In all his dressings, characts, titles, forms,
    Be an arch-villain. Believe it, royal Prince,
    If he be less, he's nothing ; but he's more,
    Had I more name for badness.
DUKE.   By mine honesty,
    If she be mad, as I believe no other,   60
    Her madness hath the oddest frame of sense,
    Such a dependency of thing on thing,
    As e'er I heard in madness.
ISAB.   O gracious Duke,
    Harp not on that ; nor do not banish reason
    For inequality ; but let your reason serve   65

Enter FRIAR THOMAS
and ISABELLA.

Throughout this scene
for 'Friar Peter' read
'Friar Thomas'.

To make the truth appear where it seems hid,
And hide the false seems true.
DUKE.   Many that are not mad
Have, sure, more lack of reason.   What would you say ?
ISAB. I am the sister of one Claudio,
Condemn'd upon the act of fornication   70
To lose his head ; condemn'd by Angelo.
I, in probation of a sisterhood,
Was sent to by my brother ; one Lucio
As then the messenger—
LUCIO.   That's I, an't like your Grace.
I came to her from Claudio, and desir'd her   75
To try her gracious fortune with Lord Angelo
For her poor brother's pardon.
ISAB.   That's he, indeed.
DUKE. You were not bid to speak.
LUCIO.   No, my good lord ;
Nor wish'd to hold my peace.
DUKE.   I wish you now, then ;
Pray you take note of it ; and when you have   80
A business for yourself, pray heaven you then
Be perfect.
LUCIO. I warrant your honour.
DUKE. The warrant's for yourself ; take heed to't.
ISAB. This gentleman told somewhat of my tale.
LUCIO. Right.   85
DUKE. It may be right ; but you are i' the wrong
To speak before your time.   Proceed.
ISAB.   I went
To this pernicious caitiff deputy.
DUKE. That's somewhat madly spoken.
ISAB.   Pardon it ;
The phrase is to the matter.   90
DUKE. Mended again.   The matter—proceed.
ISAB. In brief—to set the needless process by,
How I persuaded, how I pray'd, and kneel'd,
How he refell'd me, and how I replied,
For this was of much length—the vile conclusion   95
I now begin with grief and shame to utter :
He would not, but by gift of my chaste body
To his concupiscible intemperate lust,
Release my brother ; and, after much debatement,
My sisterly remorse confutes mine honour,   100
And I did yield to him.   But the next morn betimes,
His purpose surfeiting, he sends a warrant
For my poor brother's head.
DUKE.   This is most likely !
ISAB. O that it were as like as it is true !
DUKE. By heaven, fond wretch, thou know'st not what thou speak'st,
Or else thou art suborn'd against his honour   106
In hateful practice.   First, his integrity
Stands without blemish ; next, it imports no reason
That with such vehemency he should pursue
Faults proper to himself.   If he had so offended,   110

He would have weigh'd thy brother by himself,
And not have cut him off.   Some one hath set you on;
Confess the truth, and say by whose advice
Thou cam'st here to complain.
ISAB.   And is this all?
Then, O you blessed ministers above,   115
Keep me in patience ; and, with ripened time,
Unfold the evil which is here wrapt up
In countenance! Heaven shield your Grace from woe,
As I, thus wrong'd, hence unbelieved go!
DUKE. I know you'd fain be gone.   An officer!   120
To prison with her! Shall we thus permit
A blasting and a scandalous breath to fall
On him so near us? This needs must be a practice.
Who knew of your intent and coming hither?
ISAB. One that I would were here, friar Lodowick.   125
DUKE. A ghostly father, belike.   Who knows that Lodowick?
LUCIO. My Lord, I know him ; 'tis a meddling friar.
I do not like the man ; had he been lay, my lord,
For certain words he spake against your Grace
In your retirement, I had swing'd him soundly.   130
DUKE. Words against me? This's a good friar, belike!
And to set on this wretched woman here
Against our substitute! Let this friar be found.
LUCIO. But yesternight, my lord, she and that friar,
I saw them at the prison ; a saucy friar,   135
A very scurvy fellow.
F. PETER. Blessed be your royal Grace!
I have stood by, my lord, and I have heard
Your royal ear abus'd.   First, hath this woman
Most wrongfully accus'd your substitute ;   140
Who is as free from touch or soil with her
As she from one ungot.
DUKE.   We did believe no less.
Know you that friar Lodowick that she speaks of?
F. PETER. I know him for a man divine and holy ;
Not scurvy, nor a temporary meddler,   145
As he's reported by this gentleman ;
And, on my trust, a man that never yet
Did, as he vouches, misreport your Grace.
LUCIO. My lord, most villainously ; believe it.
F. PETER. Well, he in time may come to clear himself   150
But at this instant he is sick, my lord,
Of a strange fever.   Upon his mere request—
Being come to knowledge that there was complaint
Intended 'gainst Lord Angelo—came I hither
To speak, as from his mouth, what he doth know   155
Is true and false ; and what he, with his oath
And all probation, will make up full clear,
Whensoever he's convented.   First, for this woman—
To justify this worthy nobleman,
So vulgarly and personally accus'd—   160
Her shall you hear disproved to her eyes,
Till she herself confess it.

DUKE.   Good friar, let's hear it.
[exit ISABELLA *guarded.*
Do you not smile at this, Lord Angelo?
O heaven, the vanity of wretched fools!
Give us some seats.   Come, cousin Angelo;   165
In this I'll be impartial; be you judge
Of your own cause.

            Enter MARIANA *veiled.*

          Is this the witness, friar?
First let her show her face, and after speak.
MARI. Pardon, my lord; I will not show my face
Until my husband bid me.   170
DUKE. What, are you married?
MARI. No, my lord.
DUKE. Are you a maid?
MARI. No, my lord.
DUKE. A widow, then?   175
MARI. Neither, my lord.
DUKE. Why, you are nothing then; neither maid, widow, nor wife.
LUCIO. My lord, she may be a punk; for many of them are neither
maid, widow, nor wife.   180
DUKE. Silence that fellow.   I would he had some cause
To prattle for himself.
LUCIO. Well, my lord.
MARI. My lord, I do confess I ne'er was married,
And I confess, besides, I am no maid.   185
I have known my husband; yet my husband
Knows not that ever he knew me.
LUCIO. He was drunk, then, my lord; it can be no better.
DUKE. For the benefit of silence, would thou wert so too!
LUCIO. Well, my lord.   190
DUKE. This is no witness for Lord Angelo.
MARI. Now I come to't, my lord:
She that accuses him of fornication,
In self-same manner doth accuse my husband;
And charges him, my lord, with such a time   195
When I'll depose I had him in mine arms,
With all th' effect of love.
ANG. Charges she moe than me?
MARI.   Not that I know.
DUKE. No? You say your husband.
MARI. Why, just, my lord, and that is Angelo,   200
Who thinks he knows that he ne'er knew my body,
But knows he thinks that he knows Isabel's.
ANG. This is a strange abuse.   Let's see thy face.
MARI. My husband bids me; now I will unmask.   *[unveiling.*
This is that face, thou cruel Angelo,   205
Which once thou swor'st was worth the looking on;
This is the hand which, with a vow'd contract,
Was fast belock'd in thine; this is the body
That took away the match from Isabel,
And did supply thee at thy garden-house   210
In her imagin'd person.

DUKE.   Know you this woman ?
LUCIO. Carnally, she says.
DUKE.   Sirrah, no more.
LUCIO. Enough, my lord.
ANG. My lord, I must confess I know this woman ;
    And five years since there was some speech of marriage   215
    Betwixt myself and her ; which was broke off,
    Partly for that her promised proportions
    Came short of composition ; but in chief
    For that her reputation was disvalued
    In levity.   Since which time of five years   220
    I never spake with her, saw her, nor heard from her,
    Upon my faith and honour.
MARI.   Noble Prince,
    As there comes light from heaven and words from breath,
    As there is sense in truth and truth in virtue,
    I am affianc'd this man's wife as strongly   225
    As words could make up vows.   And, my good lord,
    But Tuesday night last gone, in's garden-house,
    He knew me as a wife.   As this is true,
    Let me in safety raise me from my knees,
    Or else for ever be confixed here,   230
    A marble monument !
ANG.   I did but smile till now.
    Now, good my lord, give me the scope of justice ;
    My patience here is touch'd.   I do perceive
    These poor informal women are no more
    But instruments of some more mightier member   235
    That sets them on.   Let me have way, my lord,
    To find this practice out.
DUKE.   Ay, with my heart ;
    And punish them to your height of pleasure.
    Thou foolish friar, and thou pernicious woman,
    Compact with her that's gone, think'st thou thy oaths,   240
    Though they would swear down each particular saint,
    Were testimonies against his worth and credit,
    That's seal'd in approbation ? You, Lord Escalus,
    Sit with my cousin ; lend him your kind pains
    To find out this abuse, whence 'tis deriv'd.   245
    There is another friar that set them on ;
    Let him be sent for.
F. PETER. Would he were here, my lord ! For he indeed
    Hath set the women on to this complaint.
    Your provost knows the place where he abides,   250
    And he may fetch him.
DUKE.   Go, do it instantly.
                                      [*exit* PROVOST.
    And you, my noble and well-warranted cousin,
    Whom it concerns to hear this matter forth,
    Do with your injuries as seems you best
    In any chastisement.   I for a while will leave you ;   255
    But stir not you till you have well determin'd
    Upon these slanderers.

ESCAL.   My lord, we'll do it throughly.
                                                   [*exit* DUKE.
Signior Lucio, did not you say you knew that Friar Lodowick to
be a dishonest person ?   260
LUCIO. ' Cucullus non facit monachum ' : honest in nothing but in
his clothes ; and one that hath spoke most villainous speeches
of the Duke.
ESCAL. We shall entreat you to abide here till he come, and enforce
them against him.   We shall find this friar a notable fellow.
LUCIO. As any in Vienna, on my word.
ESCAL. Call that same Isabel here once again ; I would speak with
her. [*Exit an* ATTENDANT] Pray you, my lord, give me leave to
question ; you shall see how I'll handle her.   271
LUCIO. Not better than he, by her own report.
ESCAL. Say you ?
LUCIO. Marry, sir, I think, if you handled her privately, she would
sooner confess ; perchance, publicly, she'll be asham'd.   276

          Re-enter OFFICERS *with* ISABELLA ; *and* PROVOST *with the*
                    DUKE *in his friar's habit.*

ESCAL. I will go darkly to work with her.
LUCIO. That's the way ; for women are light at midnight.
ESCAL. Come on, mistress ; here's a gentlewoman denies all that you
have said.   280
LUCIO. My lord, here comes the rascal I spoke of, here with the
Provost.
ESCAL. In very good time.   Speak not you to him till we call upon you.
LUCIO. Mum.   285
ESCAL. Come, sir ; did you set these women on to slander Lord
Angelo ?   They have confess'd you did.
DUKE. 'Tis false.
ESCAL. How ! Know you where you are ?
DUKE. Respect to your great place ! and let the devil   290
Be sometime honour'd for his burning throne !
Where is the Duke ?   'Tis he should hear me speak.
ESCAL. The Duke's in us ; and we will hear you speak ;
Look you speak justly.
DUKE. Boldly, at least.   But, O, poor souls,   295
Come you to seek the lamb here of the fox,
Good night to your redress ! Is the Duke gone ?
Then is your cause gone too.   The Duke's unjust
Thus to retort your manifest appeal,
And put your trial in the villain's mouth   300
Which here you come to accuse.
LUCIO. This is the rascal ; this is he I spoke of.
ESCAL. Why, thou unreverend and unhallowed friar,
Is't not enough thou hast suborn'd these women
To accuse this worthy man, but, in foul mouth,   305
And in the witness of his proper ear,
To call him villain ; and then to glance from him
To th' Duke himself, to tax him with injustice ?
Take him hence ; to th' rack with him ! We'll touze you
Joint by joint, but we will know his purpose.   310
What, ' unjust ' !

DUKE.   Be not so hot ; the Duke
Dare no more stretch this finger of mine than he
Dare rack his own ; his subject am I not,
Nor here provincial.   My business in this state
Made me a looker-on here in Vienna,   315
Where I have seen corruption boil and bubble
Till it o'errun the stew : laws for all faults,
But faults so countenanc'd that the strong statutes
Stand like the forfeits in a barber's shop,
As much in mock as mark.   320
ESCAL. Slander to th' state ! Away with him to prison !
ANG. What can you vouch against him, Signior Lucio ?
Is this the man that you did tell us of ?
LUCIO. 'Tis he, my lord. Come hither, good-man bald-pate. Do
you know me ?   325
DUKE. I remember you, sir, by the sound of your voice. I met you
at the prison, in the absence of the Duke.
LUCIO. O did you so ? And do you remember what you said of the
Duke ?
DUKE. Most notedly, sir.   330
LUCIO. Do you so, sir ? And was the Duke a fleshmonger, a fool, and
a coward, as you then reported him to be ?
DUKE. You must, sir, change persons with me ere you make that my
report ; you, indeed, spoke so of him ; and much more, much
worse.   336
LUCIO. O thou damnable fellow ! Did not I pluck thee by the nose
for thy speeches ?
DUKE. I protest I love the Duke as I love myself.
ANG. Hark how the villain would close now, after his treasonable
abuses !   341
ESCAL. Such a fellow is not to be talk'd withal. Away with him to
prison ! Where is the Provost ? Away with him to prison !
Lay bolts enough upon him ; let him speak no more.   Away with
those giglets too, and with the other confederate companion ! 346
                    [the PROVOST lays hands on the DUKE.
DUKE. Stay, sir ; stay awhile.
ANG. What, resists he ? Help him, Lucio.
LUCIO. Come, sir ; come, sir ; come, sir ; foh, sir ! Why, you
bald-pated lying rascal, you must be hooded, must you ? Show
your knave's visage, with a pox to you ! Show your sheep-biting
face, and be hang'd an hour ! Will't not off ?   353
                    [pulls off the FRIAR'S hood and discovers the DUKE.
DUKE. Thou art the first knave that e'er mad'st a duke.
First, Provost, let me bail these gentle three.   355
[to LUCIO] Sneak not away, sir, for the friar and you
Must have a word anon. Lay hold on him.
LUCIO. This may prove worse than hanging.
DUKE. [to ESCALUS] What you have spoke I pardon · sit you down.
We'll borrow place of him. [to ANGELO] Sir, by your leave. 360
Hast thou or word, or wit, or impudence,
That yet can do thee office ? If thou hast,
Rely upon it till my tale be heard,
And hold no longer out.
ANG.   O my dread lord,

I should be guiltier than my guiltiness,   365
To think I can be undiscernible,
When I perceive your Grace, like pow'r divine,
Hath look'd upon my passes.   Then, good Prince,
No longer session hold upon my shame,
But let my trial be mine own confession ;   370
Immediate sentence then, and sequent death,
Is all the grace I beg.
DUKE.   Come hither, Mariana.
Say, wast thou e'er contracted to this woman ?
ANG. I was, my lord.
DUKE. Go, take her hence and marry her instantly.   375
Do you the office, friar ; which consummate,
Return him here again.   Go with him, Provost.
      [*exeunt* ANGELO, MARIANA, FRIAR PETER, *and* PROVOST.   For 'PETER' read
ESCAL. My lord, I am more amaz'd at his dishonour   'THOMAS'.
Than at the strangeness of it.
DUKE.   Come hither, Isabel.
Your friar is now your prince.   As I was then   380
Advertising and holy to your business,
Not changing heart with habit, I am still
Attorney'd at your service.
ISAB.   O, give me pardon,
That I, your vassal, have employ'd and pain'd
Your unknown sovereignty.
DUKE.   You are pardon'd, Isabel.   385
And now, dear maid, be you as free to us.
Your brother's death, I know, sits at your heart ;
And you may marvel why I obscur'd myself,
Labouring to save his life, and would not rather
Make rash remonstrance of my hidden pow'r   390
Than let him so be lost.   O most kind maid,
It was the swift celerity of his death,
Which I did think with slower foot came on,
That brain'd my purpose.   But peace be with him !
That life is better life, past fearing death,   395
Than that which lives to fear.   Make it your comfort,
So happy is your brother.
ISAB.   I do, my lord.

    Re-enter ANGELO, MARIANA, FRIAR PETER, *and* PROVOST.   For 'PETER' read
                                                              'THOMAS'.
DUKE. For this new-married man approaching here,
Whose salt imagination yet hath wrong'd
Your well-defended honour, you must pardon   400
For Mariana's sake ; but as he adjudg'd your brother—
Being criminal in double violation
Of sacred chastity and of promise-breach,
Thereon dependent, for your brother's life—
The very mercy of the law cries out   405
Most audible, even from his proper tongue,
' An Angelo for Claudio, death for death ! '
Haste still pays haste, and leisure answers leisure ;
Like doth quit like, and Measure still for Measure.
Then, Angelo, thy fault's thus manifested,   410

Which, though thou wouldst deny, denies thee vantage.
We do condemn thee to the very block
Where Claudio stoop'd to death, and with like haste.
Away with him!
MARI.   O my most gracious lord,
I hope you will not mock me with a husband.   415
DUKE. It is your husband mock'd you with a husband.
Consenting to the safeguard of your honour,
I thought your marriage fit; else imputation,
For that he knew you, might reproach your life,
And choke your good to come. For his possessions,   420
Although by confiscation they are ours,
We do instate and widow you withal,
To buy you a better husband.
MARI.   O my dear lord,
I crave no other, nor no better man.
DUKE. Never crave him; we are definitive.   425
MARI. Gentle my liege—   [kneeling.
DUKE.   You do but lose your labour.
Away with him to death! [to LUCIO] Now, sir, to you.
MARI. O my good lord! Sweet Isabel, take my part;
Lend me your knees, and all my life to come
I'll lend you all my life to do you service.   430
DUKE. Against all sense you do importune her.
Should she kneel down in mercy of this fact,
Her brother's ghost his paved bed would break,
And take her hence in horror.
MARI.   Isabel,
Sweet Isabel, do yet but kneel by me;   435
Hold up your hands, say nothing; I'll speak all.
They say best men are moulded out of faults;
And, for the most, become much more the better
For being a little bad; so may my husband.
O Isabel, will you not lend a knee?   440
DUKE. He dies for Claudio's death.
ISAB. [kneeling.] Most bounteous sir,
Look, if it please you, on this man condemn'd,
As if my brother liv'd. I partly think
A due sincerity govern'd his deeds
Till he did look on me; since it is so,   445
Let him not die. My brother had but justice,
In that he did the thing for which he died;
For Angelo,
His act did not o'ertake his bad intent,
And must be buried but as an intent   450
That perish'd by the way. Thoughts are no subjects;
Intents but merely thoughts.
MARI.   Merely, my lord.
DUKE. Your suit's unprofitable; stand up, I say.
I have bethought me of another fault.
Provost, how came it Claudio was beheaded   455
At an unusual hour?
PROV.   It was commanded so.
DUKE. Had you a special warrant for the deed?

PROV. No, my good lord ; it was by private message.
DUKE. For which I do discharge you of your office ;
Give up your keys.
PROV.   Pardon me, noble lord ;   460
I thought it was a fault, but knew it not ;
Yet did repent me, after more advice ;
For testimony whereof, one in the prison,
That should by private order else have died,
I have reserv'd alive.
DUKE.   What's he ?
PROV.   His name is Barnardine.   465
DUKE. I would thou hadst done so by Claudio.
Go fetch him hither ; let me look upon him.   [exit PROVOST.
ESCAL. I am sorry one so learned and so wise
As you, Lord Angelo, have still appear'd,
Should slip so grossly, both in the heat of blood   470
And lack of temper'd judgment afterward.
ANG. I am sorry that such sorrow I procure ;
And so deep sticks it in my penitent heart
That I crave death more willingly than mercy ;
'Tis my deserving, and I do entreat it.   475

          Re-enter PROVOST, with BARNARDINE, CLAUDIO (muffled)
                         and JULIET.

DUKE. Which is that Barnardine ?
PROV.   This, my lord.
DUKE. There was a friar told me of this man.
Sirrah, thou art said to have a stubborn soul,
That apprehends no further than this world,
And squar'st thy life according. Thou'rt condemn'd ;   480
But, for those earthly faults, I quit them all,
And pray thee take this mercy to provide
For better times to come. Friar, advise him ;
I leave him to your hand. What muffl'd fellow's that ?
PROV. This is another prisoner that I sav'd,   485
Who should have died when Claudio lost his head ;
As like almost to Claudio as himself.   [unmuffles CLAUDIO.
DUKE. [to ISABELLA]   If he be like your brother, for his sake
Is he pardon'd ; and for your lovely sake,
Give me your hand and say you will be mine,   490
He is my brother too. But fitter time for that.
By this Lord Angelo perceives he's safe ;
Methinks I see a quick'ning in his eye.
Well, Angelo, your evil quits you well.
Look that you love your wife ; her worth worth yours.   495
I find an apt remission in myself ;
And yet here's one in place I cannot pardon.
[to LUCIO] You, sirrah, that knew me for a fool, a coward,
One all of luxury, an ass, a madman !
Wherein have I so deserv'd of you   500
That you extol me thus ?
LUCIO. Faith, my lord, I spoke it but according to the trick. If you
will hang me for it, you may ; but I had rather it would please
you I might be whipt.

DUKE. Whipt first, sir, and hang'd after. 505
Proclaim it, Provost, round about the city,
If any woman wrong'd by this lewd fellow—
As I have heard him swear himself there's one
Whom he begot with child, let her appear,
And he shall marry her. The nuptial finish'd, 510
Let him be whipt and hang'd.
LUCIO. I beseech your Highness, do not marry me to a whore. Your
Highness said even now I made you a duke ; good my lord, do
not recompense me in making me a cuckold. 515
DUKE. Upon mine honour, thou shalt marry her.
Thy slanders I forgive ; and therewithal
Remit thy other forfeits. Take him to prison ;
And see our pleasure herein executed.
LUCIO. Marrying a punk, my lord, is pressing to death, whipping,
and hanging. 521
DUKE. Slandering a prince deserves it.
[exeunt OFFICERS *with* LUCIO.
She, Claudio, that you wrong'd, look you restore.
Joy to you, Mariana ! Love her, Angelo ;
I have confess'd her, and I know her virtue. 525
Thanks, good friend Escalus, for thy much goodness ;
There's more behind that is more gratulate.
Thanks, Provost, for thy care and secrecy ;
We shall employ thee in a worthier place.
Forgive him, Angelo, that brought you home 530
The head of Ragozine for Claudio's :
Th' offence pardons itself. Dear Isabel,
I have a motion much imports your good ;
Whereto if you'll a willing ear incline,
What's mine is yours, and what is yours is mine. 535
So, bring us to our palace, where we'll show
What's yet behind that's meet you all should know.

[exeunt.

GLOSSARY

Scott Shane

Difficult phrases are listed under the most important or most difficult word in them. If no such word stands out, they are listed under the first word.

Words appear in the form they take in the text. If they occur in several forms, they are listed under the root form (singular for nouns, infinitive for verbs).

Line references are given only when the same word is used with different meanings, and when there are puns.

Line numbers for prose passages are counted from the last numbered line before the line referred to (since the numbers given follow the lines in the First Folio and not those in this edition).

ABIDE, (i) dwell (IV ii 21, V i 250); (ii) remain (V i 264)
ABSOLUTE, (i) absolutely resolved (III i 5); (ii) free from imperfection (V i 54)
ABUSE (n.), (i) corrupt practice (II i 42); (ii) false accusation, insult (V i 203, 245, 341); (v.), (i) malign, slander (III ii 191); (ii) deceive (V i 139)
ACCOMMODATIONS, comforts, endowments
ACCOMPT, 'Stand more for number than accompt', are recorded but add little to the account of our sins
ACCOUNTANT, accountable
ACKNOWLEDGE ITSELF, should become publicly known
ACTION, (i) military action (I iv 52); (ii) lawsuit (II i 171–2); 'in action all of precept', detailed directions by means of gestures
ADJUDG'D, condemned
ADVANTAGE, 'refer yourself to this advantage', impose this condition
ADVERTISE, 'my part in him advertise', instruct me in the duties of my office, which is now vested in him
ADVERTISING, attentive
ADVICE, consideration, reflection (V i 462)
AFFECT, show a foolish fondness for
AFFECTION, passion
AFFIANCED, betrothed, engaged to marry
AFOOT, begun, in process
AFTER, for the price of (II i 229)

AGED IN ANY KIND OF COURSE, of long standing in any sort of activity
ALIKE, 'all alike', just the same
ALL-HALLOND EVE, Halloween, 31 October
AMBUSH, 'in th' ambush', under the cover
AN, if
ANCIENT, former
AND, if (III ii 246)
ANON, soon, in a while
ANSWER (n.), (i) responsibility (II iv 73); (ii) statement of accusations (III ii 145); (v.), (i) be responsible to, be held responsible for (II i 39, II ii 93, 103, IV ii 119, IV iii 159); (ii) respond to (III i 234, III ii 165); (iii) correspond to, agree with (III i 238, III ii 238, V i 408)
ANTIQUITY, 'of antiquity', (i) by heritage; (ii) of long standing (pun, III ii 63)
APACE, rapidly, without deliberation
APPLIANCES, 'in base appliances', by means of base remedies
APPOINTED, arranged, given a date
APPOINTMENT, preparation
APPREHENDS, conceives, imagines
APPREHENSION, conception, imagination
APPROBATION, (i) status as a novitiate in a nunnery (I ii 171); (ii) proof and approval (V i 243)
APPROOF, approval
APT, natural
ARRAIGN, examine, interrogate
ARRAY, clothe

ARREST YOUR WORDS, take you at your word

ART, theoretical knowledge (I i 13)

ASSAULT, sexual proposition

ASSAY (n.), test, trial; (v.), (i) accost, approach (I ii 174); (ii) test, try out (I iv 76)

ATHWART, awry

ATTEMPT, win over

ATTEND, await

ATTORNEY'D, bound as an agent or attorney

AVAIL, benefit

AVES, acclamations, greetings

AVIS'D, informed

AVOID, refute, render ineffectual

AVOUCH, affirm, acknowledge

AWAKES ME, awakes, revives

AY, yes

BANE, poison

BANISH WHAT THEY SUE FOR, drive away (by provoking desire) the forbearance they plead for

BARK, strip off the bark of

BASTARD, (i) a sweet Spanish wine; (ii) illegitimate child (pun, III ii 3)

BATT'RY, physical assault

BAY, part of a house beneath a single gable

BEFELL TO, affected

BEGIN THY HEALTH, begin drinking to your health

BEGUILES, deceives

BEHIND, to come

BEHOLDING, beholden, indebted

BELIKE, it seems, apparently

BELOCK'D, locked

BELONGINGS, capabilities

BEND, direct

BENEDICITE, bless you

BETHINK (YOU, ME), consider, reflect

BETIMES, early

BILLETS, sticks of wood

BITE . . . BY TH' NOSE, treat with contempt, mock

BLASTING, withering, ruinous

BLENCH, deviate

BLISTER'D HER REPORT, marred her reputation

BLOOD, passion, sexual desire

BODY PUBLIC, citizenry

BOLTS, fetters, shackles

BONDS, obligations

BOOT, 'with boot', profitably

BORE . . . IN HAND, AND HOPE, deceived with the hope

BORNE UP, supported, made plausible

BOSOM, heart's desire

BOTTOM OF MY PLACE, character of my office

BOWELS, 'thine own bowels', i.e. your own children

BRAIN'D, killed, thwarted

BRAN, very coarse bread; 'water and bran', a diet designed to curb sexual desire

BRAVERY, 'witless bravery', senseless display

BRAWLING, clamorous, noisy

BREAKS, 'run from breaks of ice', i.e. are cold-blooded and cold-hearted

BREATHER, 'But it confounds the breather', without confounding the utterer (of the scandal)

BRING YOU SOMETHING ON, escort you part of

BRINGINGS-FORTH, achievements

BROTHER, fellow ruler (III ii 194, 196)

BUNCH OF GRAPES, name of a room at a tavern

BURGHER, well-to-do citizen

CAITIFF, wretch, villain

CALL YOU, call on you

CALUMNY, slander

CARDINALLY, Elbow's mistake for 'carnally'

CARMAN, cart-driver

CARRION, decaying flesh

CARRY, perform, succeed in

CASE, outward appearance

CAST, dug out, cleansed (of a ditch or pond)

CAUSE, legal dispute or accusation

CELERITY, speed; 'quick celerity', living speed, i.e. encouragement

CENSURE, pass sentence upon

CERTAIN, constant, reliable

CHARACTER, handwriting

CHARACTERS, letters

CHARACTS, insignia of office

CHARGE, command, order

CHEAP, 'the goodness that is cheap in beauty', the ability to please which comes so easily to a beautiful woman

CHIEF, 'in chief', chiefly

CHOLERIC, angry

CIPHER, zero; 'Mine were the very cipher of a function', I would be utterly neglecting my duty

CIRCUMMUR'D, walled round

CLACK-DISH, beggar's wooden bowl (with sexual suggestion)

CLAP INTO, begin quickly

CLOSE (adj.), silent; (v.), come to terms, compromise

CLUTCH'D, i.e. grasping money

COAT, clerical dress

CODPIECE, pouch in trousers covering genitals; thus, genitals

COFFER, strongbox for the storage of money and other valuables

COLOUR, disguise

COMBINATE, betrothed

COMBINED, bound

COME, 'come me to', come to; 'he's coming', he's yielding; 'come your way(s)', come along

COMMODITY, goods lent for resale; Master Rash borrowed 'five marks' (just over three pounds) and the goods from a usurer, who valued the goods at 'nine score and seventeen pounds' and was thus able to charge an effective rate of interest far higher than the legal maximum of 10%

COMMON RIGHT, 'Do me the common right', allow me the right common to all clergymen

COMMUNE, confer

COMPACT, leagued, conspiring

COMPELL'D, involuntary

COMPLETE, (i) perfect in nature; (ii) fully equipped, armoured

COMPLEXION, character, temperament

COMPOSITION, (i) agreement (I ii 1); (ii) the sum agreed upon (V i 218)

COMPOUND, come to terms

CONCEPTION, plan, design

CONCERNINGS, concerns

CONCUPISCIBLE, strongly desirous

CONDITION, necessity

CONFESS'D HER, heard her confession

CONFIXED, fixed firmly

CONFUTES, confounds, defeats

CONJURE, call upon solemnly

CONSENTING TO, having regard for

CONSTANTLY, certainly, assuredly

CONSUMMATE, concluded

CONTENDED, attempted

CONTINENCY, sexual continence

CONTINUE, (i) Elbow's apparent mistake for 'contain', i.e. be continent (II i 181-2); (ii) preserve, allow to live (IV iii 80)

CONTRARIOUS, 'most contrarious quest', hunt in the wrong direction

CONVENTED, summoned

COPPERSPUR, owner of cheap copper spurs meant to simulate gold

CORD, belt of friar's habit (compared to hangman's noose)

CORNERS, 'of dark corners', suggesting (i) the duke's supposed personal sexual laxness, and (ii) the duke's supposed secret political work abroad

COUNTENANCE, 'wrapt up In countenance', (i) allowed by authority, countenanced; (ii) concealed by hypocritical pretence

COUNTERMAND, reprieve

COURSE, conduct, procedure; 'in course', in turn; 'pervert your course', subvert your success

COUSIN, (i) relative (I iv 45-6); (ii) form of address used by a ruler to a nobleman (V i 1, 165, 244, 252)

COVENT, convent, monastery

CRABBED, harsh, severe

CRAVE, beg, seek

CREDENT BULK, weight of credibility, capacity for being believed

CREDITORS, 'send for certain of my creditors', i.e. so as to be arrested for debt and thus be able to 'speak so wisely' as Claudio

CREDULOUS TO FALSE PRINTS, susceptible to illegitimate advances

CREST, heraldic symbol; i.e. proper designation

CROSS, (i) are at cross purposes (II ii 159); (ii) hinder, disobey (IV ii 159)

CROTCHETS, whims, fancies

CRY YOU MERCY, beg your pardon

CUCULLUS NON FACIT MONACHUM, a hood does not make a monk (proverbial for 'appearances are deceptive')

CUNNING, skill, knowledge

CURFEW, evening bell of the prison

CURTSY, 'make curtsy to', i.e. bow down before, obey

CUSTOM-SHRUNK, short of customers

CUT OFF, executed

DARKLY, (i) secretly (III ii 165); (ii) slyly, cunningly (V i 277)

DEAD TO INFLICTION, never enforced

DEBATEMENT, indecision, vacillation

DEDICATE, dedicated

DEEPVOW, a swearer

DEFINITIVE, irrevocably resolved

DEGREES, stages of life

DELIGHTED, capable of delight

DELIVER, communicate, disclose; 'deliver me', deliver for me

DENUNCIATION, public announcement

DEPENDANT, 'your free dependant', willingly at your service

DEPENDENCY OF THING ON THING, logical succession of ideas

DEPENDING, dependant, parasitic

DEPOSE, declare under oath

DEPUTATION, position as deputy

DEPUTED SWORD, emblematic sword of justice given to an official

DESIRE, ask, request

DESPITE OF, in spite of

DETECTED FOR, accused for behaviour with

DETERMIN'D UPON, decided the fate of

DETEST, Elbow's mistake for 'protest'

DEVICES, contrived charges

DISCOVER, uncover, expose; 'discover the favour', recognise the face

DISMISS'D, pardoned

DISPATCH (n.), rapid settlement; (v.), perform an action, or settle an affair, with haste

DISPENSE WITH, (i) grant a dispensation for, condone (III i 136); (ii) forgo, give up (III i 155)

DISPOSE OF HER, have her moved

DISPOSITION, 'practise his judgment with the disposition of natures', try out his ability as a judge of character

DISSOLUTION, death, destruction

DISTRACTED, mad, mentally unbalanced

DISVALUED IN LEVITY, discredited because of moral levity

DISVOUCH'D OTHER, contradicted the rest

DIVINES, clergymen

DIZY, possibly meant to suggest 'dizzy', i.e. foolish

DO IN SLANDER, be discredited

DOLOURS, painful illnesses (with pun on 'dollars', I ii 48)

DOOM, sentence

DOW'R, dowry

DRABS, prostitutes

DRAW, (i) draw liquor from a cask; i.e. empty; (ii) put to death by disembowelling (pun, II i 194)

DRESSINGS, robes of office

DRIBBLING, feeble, falling short of the mark

DRIFT, plan

DROPHEIR, either (i) one who preys on young heirs; or (ii) a young heir who has squandered his inheritance

DUCAT, gold coin (with sexual suggestion)

DUKES IT, plays the duke

DURANCE, imprisonment

EFFECT, (i) accomplishment (II i 13); (ii) appearance, outward manifestation (III i 24, V i 197); (iii) demonstration (IV ii 151)

EFFUSION, 'mere effusion of thy proper loins', your offspring

ELBOW, 'he's out at elbow', i.e. he has worn out his wit (with pun)

ELD, old age

ELECTED, chosen

ENEMY, Satan

ENEW, drive into the water

ENFORCE, assert vigorously, emphasise

ENROLLED, written on a roll of parchment

ENSHIELDED, shielded, veiled

ENSKIED, placed in heaven

ENTERTAIN, maintain

ENTERTAINMENT, reception

ENVY, malice, hatred

ERRAND, 'he were as good go a mile on his errand', i.e. he'll be punished severely

ESCAPES, sallies

ESTIMATION, reputation

EVEN, evening

EVENTS, 'his events', the outcome of his affairs

EVERMORE, all along, always

EVILS, possibly 'privies'; more likely 'evil structures' (II ii 172)

EXACTING, 'Pay with falsehood false exacting', pay back by means of a disguise Angelo's dishonest exaction of sexual favours

EXPRESS'D, revealed, shown to be

EXTIRP, extirpate, exterminate

FACING, 'stands for the facing', supports the outer covering

FACT, crime

FAIN, (i) obliged (IV iii 149, 166); (ii) gladly (V i 15, 21, 120)

FALL, let fall (II i 6); 'falls out,' occurs; 'fall to you upon this', happen to you because of this

FALLOW, field formerly left bare of crops

FANCY, whimsical imagination

FANTASTIC (adj.), capricious, grotesque; (n.), one who indulges in fanciful ideas or in showy dress

FANTASTICAL, capricious, whimsical

FAST MY WIFE, my wife by virtue of 'handfasting', an exchange of pledges recognised as marriage under English common law, though the church required a religious ceremony

FAVOUR, (i) friendly regard, approval (V i 16); (ii) face, appearance (IV ii 165); (pun on (i) and (ii), IV ii 26)

FEAR, frighten (II i 2); 'fear not you', do not fear

FEDARY, confederate, fellow-man

FEVEROUS, feverish

FEW, 'in few', in short

FEWNESS AND TRUTH, briefly and truly

FIGURE, 'What figure of us think you he will bear?', how do you think he will, as my deputy, represent me?

FIGURING, imagining

FILE, 'the greater file of the subject', the majority of his subjects

FINE (n.), punishment (implying that the faults have been punished by being recorded as faults); (v.), (i) punish (III i 116); (ii) bring to an end (pun on (i) and (ii), II ii 40)

FIT, prepare morally and spiritually

FLAT, downright, sheer

FLAWS, gusts of passion

FLESHMONGER, fornicator

FLOURISH, embellish, adorn

FOISON, harvest

FOLLIES, sins of lust, wantonness

FOND, (i) trivial, trifling (II ii 149); (ii) foolish (V i 105); (iii) tender, affectionate (pun on (ii) and (iii), I iii 23, II ii 187)

FONDNESS, foolish affection

FOPPERY, foolishness

FOR THE LORD'S SAKE, the cry of prisoners begging from passers-by

FOR THEM, as their deputy (II i 256)

FORBEARANCE, withdrawal, absence

FORCE, enforce

FORERUNNING, preceding, promising

FORFEIT (n.), (i) penalty, punishment (I iv 66, V i 518); (ii) offender to be punished (II ii 71, IV ii 150); 'forfeits in a barber shop', probably a list of comic penalties for bad manners and other offences on the part of customers; (adj.), guilty, condemned by law

FORGIVENESS, 'he doth oftener ask forgiveness', i.e. of the condemned man (a customary practice of the hangman)

FORK, forked tongue

FORMALLY, in outward appearance

FORMS, (i) reflections (II iv 126); (ii) ceremonies (V i 56)

FORSWEAR, deny, repudiate

FORSWORN, perjured

FORTED, fortified

FORTH, through to the end (V i 253)

FRAME (v.), (i) prepare (III i 244); (ii) devise, conceive (III ii 229)

FRAME OF SENSE, appearance of sanity

FRANKLY, unrestrainedly, unhesitatingly

FREE, generous (V i 386)

FRENCH CROWN, (i) coin worth seven shillings; (ii) bald head, resulting from treatment for 'the French disease', syphilis (pun, I ii 50)

FRENCH VELVET, (i) very fine kind of velvet; (ii) 'the French disease', syphilis (pun, I ii 33)

FRETTING, distressing, wearing

FRIENDS, relatives (I ii 144)

FULL, 'at full', in every respect

FURR'D GOWN, see GOWN

GAOLER, jailer

GENERAL SUBJECT, common people

GENERATION, 'under generation', people living on the other side of the world

GENEROUS, of noble birth

GETTING, begetting of

GHOSTLY FATHER, spiritual father, confessor (with pun on the meaning 'non-existent father', V i 126)

GIGLETS, loose women, wantons

GLANCE FROM, glance off (like a weapon)

GLASS, magic glass or crystal used for prophecy

GLASSES, mirrors

GLASSY ESSENCE, (i) fragile nature; (ii) nature which mirrors that of God; (iii) nature as revealed in a mirror (all or any of these meanings are possible)

GLIMPSE, flash, momentary brightness

GO TO, an expression of disapproval or impatience

GONE, 'Tuesday night last gone', last Tuesday night

GOOD TIME, 'in (very) good time', very well

GOOD-MAN, form of address used to men below the rank of gentleman

GOT, begot

GOVERNMENT, (i) way of governing; (ii) moral conduct, self-control (pun, III i 191)

GOWN, 'furr'd gown . . . fox on lambskins too', the customary dress for money-lenders in Shakespeare's time

GRACIOUS, righteous, godly

GRADATION, 'By cold gradation and well-balanc'd form', by deliberate steps and with proper observance of form

GRANGE, 'moated grange', country house surrounded by a moat

GRATULATE, gratifying

GRAVEL HEART, i.e. hard-hearted man

'GREED, agreed

GROANING, i.e. in labour
GROSS, evident(ly), obvious(ly)
GROSSLY, (i) stupidly (III i 18); (ii) flagrantly (V i 470)
GUARD, 'at a guard with', on guard against
GUARDS, trimmings on a garment
GUESS NOT, cannot guess
GYVES, shackles, fetters

HABIT, (i) monk's attire (I iii 46, III i 176); (ii) dress (II iv 13, IV v 1 (SD), V i 382)
HALFCAN, possibly a tapster who marked false capacities on his ale-pots (i.e. 'stabb'd Pots')
HALLOWMAS, All Saints' Day, 1 November
HAND, handwriting
HANGING LOOK, (i) downcast expression; (ii) look of a hangman (pun, IV ii 27)
HANNIBAL, Elbow's mistake for 'cannibal'
HAPPILY, perhaps
HEAD (n.), 'to the head of', face to face with; 'for my head', for fear of being beheaded; (v.), behead
HEAT, warmth of blood, desire
HEAVILY, grievously, sorrowfully
HEAVY SENSE, oppressive import
HELMED, steered, directed
HENT, taken their places at
HOLD (v.), 'Hold, therefore', therefore hold power as deputy: 'Hold you there', stick to this resolution; 'lies much in your holding up', depends greatly on your perseverance and support
HOLDS (n.), cells
HOLINESS, 'his Holiness', the Pope
HOLLOWLY, falsely, insincerely
HOLY, devoted
HOME, HOME AND HOME, thoroughly, effectually
HOT-HOUSE, bath-house (frequently a front for a brothel)
HOUSE OF PROFESSION, brothel
HOUSES, 'houses of resort', 'common houses', brothels; 'of two houses', completely different things
HUSBAND, (i) housekeeper; (ii) husband (pun, III ii 65)
HUSBANDRY, (i) cultivation of the soil; (ii) state of being a husband (pun, I iv 44)

IDLE, 'in idle price', useless and foolish
IMAGE, idea, conception
IMPORTS NO REASON, does not make any sense

IMPORTUNE, require
IMPOSITION, accusation
INCERTAIN, 'lawless and incertain thought', wild and unauthorised conjecture
INDIRECTLY, evasively, unstraightforwardly
INEQUALITY, 'for inequality', because my rank is not equal to Angelo's
INFLICTION, 'dead to infliction', never enforced
INFORMAL, mentally disturbed, crazy
INGOTS, bars of gold or silver
INJUNCTIONS, authoritative reasons
INSENSIBLE OF, with no concern about
INSTANCE, evidence, information
INSTATE, endow
INVENTION, imagination, thought
INVEST, clothe, dress
INWARD, intimate acquaintance
ISSUES, 'But to fine issues', except for the purpose that they may produce something fine

JADE, poor horse
JOT, bit
JOURNAL, daily
JUSTICE OR INIQUITY, stock characters in morality plays (here, 'Elbow or Pompey')

KEEP, dwell
KEEP THE HOUSE, (i) see to household affairs; (ii) stay at home (pun, III ii 66)
KERSEY, plain, coarse cloth
KIND, 'forfeit in the same kind', guilty of the same offence
KNAVE, menial servant (as well as a general term of abuse) (V i 354)
KNOW, know sexually, have sexual relations with (V i 186, 187, 201, 202, 228, 419)

LAPWING, bird which runs about to divert attention from its nest; thus jester, deceiver
LAY, a layman, not a cleric
LEAGUE, about three miles
LEAVEN'D, slowly rising, like leavened bread; i.e. carefully considered
LEIGER, resident ambassador
LEVITY, moral levity, wantonness
LIEF, 'as lief', as gladly
LIGHT, wanton, morally lax
LIGHTNESS, loose behaviour, laxness
LIKE (adj.), (i) similar; (ii) likely (V i 104); 'like you', in your place; (v.), please
LIKENESS, MADE IN CRIMES, the appearance of virtue, used in crimes

LIMB, strength of limb

LIMIT OF THE SOLEMNITY, date set for the marriage ceremony

LIMITED, fixed, specified

LINE, 'full line', full extent

LIST, (i) limit (I i 6); (ii) selvage or border of cloth discarded as waste (I ii 27, 30)

LIVERY, (i) 'destin'd livery', predestined uniform; i.e. woman's frailty (II iv 138); (ii) the dispensing of uniforms to retainers or servants (III i 96)

LIVES NOT IN THEM, is not to be found in them; i.e. they are false

LONGING HAVE BEEN SICK FOR, I have been sick with longing for

LONGS, belongs

LOOK, 'look to', expect to; 'look (that) you', see that you; 'so look'd after', watched so closely

LOSE, waste

LOWER CHAIR, possibly an easy chair at a tavern reserved for the sick but frequently usurped by the lazy

LUXURY, lust

MAID, virgin (with pun on the meaning 'young fish', I ii 88)

MAKE, 'made them for us', made them consent to our marriage; 'make me know', let me know; 'made a man', i.e. given new life; 'mad'st a duke', invested a man with the title of duke

MANIFEST, of obvious justice (V i 299)

MANIFESTED, 'in a manifested effect', by means of a clear demonstration

MARBLE, 'a marble to', i.e. totally unaffected by

MARK (n.), (i) sum of thirteen shillings and four pence (IV iii 5); (ii) serious attention (V i 320); (v.), take note of, pay attention to

MARR'D ALL ELSE, ruined everything otherwise

MARRY, indeed

MARVELLOUS LITTLE, very little

MASKS, 'these black masks', nuns' veils

MATCH, appointment

MATTER, 'to the matter', to the point, pertinent

MEAL'D, spotted, stained

MEAN, way

MEANS, (i) means, efforts; (ii) pimp, go-between (pun on (i) and (ii), II i 80); (iii) provisions and conditions for living (II ii 24)

MEASURE, (i) treatment meted out (III ii 227, V i 409); (ii) moderation (both (i) and (ii) are probably intended in the title)

MEDLAR, a kind of pear; slang for 'prostitute'

MEET, appropriate, wise

MEMBER, participant in a plot

MERCER, textile merchant

MERE, 'mere effusion', unmodified product, offspring; 'mere request', personal request

MERELY, absolutely, entirely

METHINKS, it seems to me

METTLE, (i) spirit; (ii) metal of shackles worn in prison (pun, III ii 70)

MILE, 'he were as good go a mile on his errand', i.e. he'll be punished severely

MINE, my concern (II ii 12)

MINISTER (v.), direct

MINISTERS (n.), 'blessed ministers above', angels

MISCARRIED, came to destruction

MISPLACES, puts words in the wrong places

MOCK ME WITH A HUSBAND, i.e. give me a husband simply to take him away

MOE, more

MORE, 'at our more leisure', when we have more time

MORROW, morning

MORTAL, 'laugh mortal', either (i) laugh like ordinary mortals; or (ii) laugh themselves to death; 'desperately mortal', in a desperate state of mortal sin

MORTALITY, (i) the power of sentencing to death (I i 45); (ii) the realm of mortality, human life (III ii 172); (iii) death (IV ii 137)

MOST, 'my most stay', my longest possible stay; 'for the most', for the most part

MOTHER, prioress, head of the nunnery

MOTION, (i) prompting (I iv 59); (ii) power of movement of the blood and body (III ii 121); (iii) 'motion generative', male puppet (III ii 103); (iv) proposal (V i 533)

MOUTH WITH, kiss erotically

MUCH, great (V i 526)

MUCH UPON THIS TIME, at about this time

MUSTER TO, gather in (possibly with suggestion of military drum, i.e. heart-beat)

MUTTON, slang for 'prostitute'

MYSTERY, profession

NAUGHTY, wicked

NEAR UPON, soon

NERVES, sinews

NEW MADE, redeemed, restored to innocence

NICETY, reserve, shyness
NINE YEARS OLD, of nine years' standing
NIPS YOUTH I' THE' HEAD, checks youth from above (like a falcon swooping on its prey)
NOR . . . NOR, neither . . . nor
NOTABLE FELLOW, notorious scoundrel
NOTEDLY, precisely
NOTHING, in no way (II iv 113)
NUMBER, 'Stand more for number than accompt', are recorded but add little to the account of our sins

OBSERVANCE, prescribed behaviour
OBSTRUCTION, immobility, *rigor mortis*
ODDS, 'makes these odds all even', levels all these inequalities, ends all these troubles
OF, possessed of (II i 185)
OFFENCEFUL, sinful
OFFICE, service (V i 362)
OMIT, ignore
ON'T, of it (II ii 132)
OPEN, public (II i 124); 'open made', disclosed, revealed
OPPOSITE, opponent
OR . . . OR, either . . . or
ORDER, 'take order for', take care of, attend to
ORGANS, instruments
OTHER SOME, others
OUTSTRETCH'D, opened wide
OWE, possess; 'As they themselves would owe them', as if they themselves could grant them

PACE, direct
PAIN, penalty
PAINT, apply cosmetics
PAINTING, (i) the art of painting (IV ii 32); (ii) cosmetics (IV ii 33)
PALSIED, either (i) paralysed; or (ii) trembling
PARCELBAWD, part-time bawd
PART, 'their own part', their own places
PARTIAL, 'nothing come in partial', let no partiality be shown toward me
PARTICULAR, (i) personal (IV iv 25); (ii) individual, separate (V i 241)
PASS ON, pass sentence on
PASSES, trespasses
PAST IT, i.e. too old for sexual activity
PATTERN IN HIMSELF TO KNOW, to find the precedents for his judgements in his own behaviour
PATTERN OUT, be a pattern for
PAVED BED, grave covered with slab of stone

PAY DOWN, pay
PEACHES HIM, denounces him as
PECULIAR, private
PELTING, paltry, insignificant
PENDENT, suspended in space
PENURY, poverty, destitution
PERADVENTURE, by chance, perhaps
PERDURABLY, eternally
PERFECT (adj.), fully prepared
PERFECT HIM WITHAL, inform him of completely
PERSUASION, belief (IV i 45)
PERVERT YOUR COURSE, subvert your success
PETITION . . . THAT PRAYS FOR PEACE, the ending of the regular grace of Shakespeare's time, 'send us peace in Christ'
PHILIP AND JACOB, the festival of St Philip and St James, 1 May
PHYSIC, medicine
PICKLOCK, an instrument for picking locks (possibly referring to chastity belts)
PIL'D, (i) having a nap, or thick, soft surface; (ii) afflicted with haemorrhoids; (iii) bald as a result of treatment for venereal disease (puns, I ii 33)
PIN, 'not of a pin', not a bit
PITH, 'my pith of business', the essence of my business
PLACE, office, position of authority; 'in his place', in the nature of his office; 'in place', at hand
PLAIN DEALING, frank speech
PLANCHED, made of planks
PLEASANT, joking
PLEASE, if it please (II iv 64, 67)
PLUCK, 'pluck . . . by the nose', openly defy, treat with contempt; 'pluck'd down', torn down; 'pluck on', test by inciting or luring
PLUME, 'idle plume', i.e. symbol of a vain and idle pleasure-seeker
POINT, 'to the point', in every detail
POISE, balance
POMPEY THE GREAT, Roman statesman and general, defeated by Julius Caesar
POSE, put a question to
POSSESS'D, informed
POSTERN, small door
POTENCY, power
POWDER'D, salted like beef, pickled
POX, 'A pox o' your throats', damn your throats; 'a pox to you', damn you
PRACTICE, deceit, conspiracy; 'make a practice', impose on, deceive

PRECEPT, 'In action all of precept', detailed directions by means of gestures

PRECISE, strict in morals, puritanical

PRE-CONTRACT, betrothal, contract of marriage

PREFERS, presents

PREFIX'D, fixed previously

PREGNANT, (i) well-versed (I i 12); (ii) obvious, apparent (II i 23)

PRESENT, immediate

PRESENTLY, immediately

PRESERVED SOULS, souls protected from the sinful world, i.e. nuns

PRESSING TO DEATH, being crushed to death by heavy weights (the punishment for a felon who refused to speak)

PRETENDING, falsely alleging

PRICE, 'in idle price', useless and foolish

PRINTS, 'credulous to false prints', susceptible to illegitimate advances

PRITHEE, ask you

PROBATION, (i) period as a novitiate in a nunnery (V i 72); (ii) proof (V i 157)

PROCLAIM, denounce publicly (II iv 151)

PROCLAMATION, reputation (III ii 133)

PROCURE, cause

PROFESS, (i) take as an occupation (II i 63); (ii) attempt (III ii 222); (iii) declare, announce (IV ii 96); (iv) take as patron saint of a religious order (IV ii 170)

PROFITING BY, taking advantage of

PROGRESS, 'in progress', in due course

PROLIXIOUS, tedious, time-wasting

PROMPTURE, prompting, impulse

PRONE, either (i) eager, apt; or (ii) in a posture of helpless, submissive entreaty

PROPAGATION, augmentation, increase

PROPER, (i) exclusively (I i 31); (ii) own, very (I ii 123, III i 30, V i 306, V i 406); (iii) applicable (V i 110)

PROPERTIES, essential qualities

PROPORTION, metrical form

PROPORTIONS, marriage portion, dowry

PROVINCIAL, subject to the local laws

PROVOK'ST, summon, invoke

PROVOST, officer in charge of the imprisonment and execution of criminals

PUDDING, sausage

PUNK, prostitute

PUT, 'put to know', informed; 'put in for', interceded on behalf of; 'put these sayings upon', apply these sayings to; 'put down', suppressed, abolished; 'puts . . . to't', presses to the wall, drives to extremities

PUTTING-ON, urging, incitement

PYGMALION'S IMAGES, i.e. prostitutes (Pygmalion's sculpture, according to classical mythology, came to life when he fell in love with it)

QUALIFY, (i) mitigate, modify (I i 66); (ii) control, subdue (IV ii 79)

QUALITY, rank and occupation

QUESTION, 'first in question', first appointed; 'in the loss of question', there being no other alternative

QUICKENING, return of life

QUIT, (i) abandon (II iv 28); (ii) pardon (V i 481); (iii) requite (V i 409, 494)

RACE, (i) natural disposition; (ii) herd of horses kept for breeding (pun, II iv 160)

RACK (n.), an instrument of torture; (v.), (i) twist out of shape (as on the rack, IV i 63); (ii) torture on the rack (V i 313)

RANK, foul, lustful

RATE, values, worths

RATHER, 'the rather', the sooner, the more quickly

RAVIN DOWN, gulp greedily

RAZE, (i) erase (I ii 11); (ii) destroy, tear down (II ii 171)

RAZURE, erasure, obliteration

REBATE, make dull

REDELIVER, hand over, give back

REFELL'D, refuted, refused

REFER YOURSELF TO THIS ADVANTAGE, impose this condition

REMISSION, 'apt remission', inclination to pardon

REMISSNESS NEW, future leniency

REMIT, pardon

REMONSTRANCE, demonstration

REMORSE, compassion

REMOVE, absence

REPAIR, passage, approach

REPORT, (i) reputation (II iii 12); (ii) rumour (IV i 59)

REQUITAL, 'more requital', further reward

RESEMBLANCE, likelihood

RESOLVE, (i) answer once and for all (III i 187); (ii) reassure, dispel the doubts of (IV ii 196)

RESPECT, value, take into account

RESPECTED, Elbow's and Pompey's mistake for 'suspected'

RESPITE (n.), postponement, delay

RESPITES ME A LIFE, grants a reprieve for my life

REST, 'There rest', continue in that way of thinking

RESTRAINED, prohibited

RETORT, turn aside, reject

RHEUM, head cold

SALT, lecherous, lustful

SAUCY SWEETNESS, lecherous enjoyment

SAY YOU?, what's that you're saying?

SCALED, weighed, tested

SCAPE, escape

SCIATICA, pain in the hip or thigh (symptom of venereal disease)

SCIENCE, knowledge

SCOPE, (i) liberty, licence (I ii 121, I iii 35); (ii) space in which to move or act (I i 65, III i 71, V i 232)

SCRUPLE, (i) minute quantity (I i 38); (ii) doubt, hesitation (I i 65)

SCURVY, loathsome

SEAL'D IN APPROBATION, (i) confirmed by proof; (ii) ratified by (the duke's) approval

SEA-MAID, mermaid

SEASON, 'of season', in season; 'virtuous season', sunny weather

SECONDARY, subordinate

SECTS, classes of people

SECURITY ENOUGH TO MAKE FELLOWSHIPS ACCURST, i.e. endorsing bonds on behalf of friends ruins many friendships

SEE, the Holy See, the court of the Pope

SEED, 'stand for seed', be allowed to remain to preserve the species (with sexual suggestion)

SEEDNESS, sowing of the seed

SEEMING, dissembling

SELF-SAME, the very same

SENSE, (i) sensuality, sensual nature (I iv 59, II ii 169); (ii) meaning, import (I iv 65, V i 224); (iii) intention (IV iv 27); (iv) power of reasoning, sanity (V i 47, 61, 431); (pun on (i) and (ii), II ii 142, II iv 74)

SENSIBLE, sentient, capable of sensation

SEQUENT, subsequent, immediately following

SERE, dry, withered

SERPIGO, skin disease

SERVICE, i.e. trade of prostitution; 'worn your eyes almost out in the service', become almost as blind as Cupid (traditionally pictured on the sign in front of a brothel) working as a bawd

SET, 'set on', (i) set forth (III i 62); (ii) incite, put another person up to something (V i 112, 132, 236, 246, 249, 286); 'set me to 't', arouse my sexual desire; 'set the needless process by', make a long story short

SETTLED, composed, calm

SEVERAL, separate

SHADOW, darkness

SHEARS, 'there went but a pair of shears between us', i.e. we were cut from the same cloth

SHEEP-BITING, i.e. like a wolf in sheep's clothing, or a dog that bites the sheep it should protect

SHIELD, grant that (or, possibly, 'forbid') (III i 142)

SHOOTIE, possibly 'shoe-tie', ridiculing the elaborately ornamented footwear popular with travellers

SHORE OF MY MODESTY, limit of propriety

SHREWD, harsh, sharp

SHRIFT, confession and absolution

SHY, reserved, wary

SICLES, shekels, i.e. coins

SIEGE, seat

SIGNET, seal

SINEW, i.e. mainstay, major part

SINISTER, unjust

SIRRAH, form of address used to inferiors

SITH, since

SKINS THE VICE O' TH' TOP, covers over the vice without healing it

SKYEY INFLUENCES, influences of the stars

SLIP, scion, cutting of a plant

SMELT, smelt of

SNATCHES, wisecracks, quibbles

SNOW-BROTH, melted snow

SOMETHING, somewhat; 'something on', part of

SOMEWHAT OF, part of

SOOTH, 'in good sooth', certainly

SORT, 'men of sort and suit', men of high rank who are ordinarily attendant on the duke

SOUL, 'special soul', particular confidence or conviction

SOUND, resounding (I ii 53)

SPARE, refrain from offending

SPECIAL SOUL, particular confidence or conviction

SPEEDED, expedited

SPLAY, castrate

SPLEENS, considered to be the seat of laughter in the human constitution

SQUAR'ST, regulate, direct
STAGE ME, display myself
STAGGER IN, am uncertain
STAMPS, 'coin heaven's image In stamps that are forbid', i.e. beget illegitimate children
STAND (n.), position for standing
STANDS FOR THE FACING, supports the outer covering
STAR, 'unfolding star', morning star (indicating that it is time to release the sheep from the fold)
STARKLY, stiffly
STARVELACKEY, one who underpays his servants
STATE, statecraft
STAY, wait
STEAD, assist; 'stead up your appointment', keep your appointment for you
STEELED, hardened
STEW, (i) cauldron containing a stew; (ii) brothel (pun, V i 317)
STEW'D PRUNES, slang for 'prostitutes' (thus Pompey's apologetic 'saving your honour's reverence')
STILL, continually, always
STINGS, carnal desires
STOCK-FISHES, dried cod
STONES, gems
STORY, laughing-stock, butt of a joke
STRAIGHT, immediately
STRAITNESS, strictness
STRANGE, (i) unfamiliar, unknown (IV ii 182); (ii) strangely (V i 36–7)
STREW'D, scattered
STRICTURE, strictness
STROKE AND LINE, stroke and line of a pen, i.e. scrupulous precision (with possible puns on 'stroke' of the executioner's axe and 'line' of the hangman's noose)
STUCK, fixed
SUBJECT, subjects of a state, populace
SUBJECTS, 'Thoughts are no subjects', thoughts are not subject to legal responsibility and punishment
SUBORN'D, induced (to perform criminal act)
SUBSCRIBE NOT, do not agree to
SUBSTITUTE, deputy, i.e. Angelo
SUCCEED, inherit
SUE, plead, entreat; 'To sue', in suing
SUFFERANCE, suffering, pain
SUFFICIENCY, competence, ability (there are probably one or more lines missing between I i 9 and 10)
SUFFICIENT, capable, able

SUPPLY, gratify, satisfy the desires of (V i 210)
SUPPOS'D, Pompey's mistake for 'deposed', sworn
SUPPOSED (n.), hypothetical person
SURFEITING, 'His purpose surfeiting', having achieved his purpose
SWAY, rule
SWEAT, sweating sickness, a form of plague
SWERVE, deviate
SWING'D, thrashed

TAINTED, (i) infected with venereal disease (I ii 41); (ii) impaired (IV iv 3)
TAPHOUSE, tavern
TAPSTER, tavern-keeper, bartender
TARRY, wait
TAX, accuse, criticise
TEMPER, temperament, temperate nature
TEMPORARY MEDDLER, meddler in temporal (i.e. secular) affairs
TENDER DOWN, offer (for beheading)
TERMS, 'terms for common justice', the conditions and terminology applied in the administration of common law; 'terms of death', sentence of death
TESTED GOLD, pure gold (tested by a touchstone)
TESTIMONIED IN, judged on the basis of
THREE-PIL'D, THREEPILE, having a triple pile or nap (the thick, soft surface of velvet or other fine cloth); thus, very fine
THRILLING, piercingly cold
THROUGHLY, thoroughly
TICKLE, unsteadily, precariously
TICK-TACK, a kind of backgammon in which pegs were placed in holes to indicate the score (with sexual suggestion)
TIE THE BEARD, (possibly) trim the beard
TILTER, jouster, fighter
TILTH, tillage, cultivation
TITHE, i.e. seed-corn to produce crop from which the tithe would be paid to the church
TONGUE, denounce
TOOK, struck
TOP OF JUDGMENT, supreme judge
TOUCH (n.), sexual contact
TOUCH'D (v.), (i) endowed (I i 36); (ii) affected (IV ii 134)
TOUZE, tear
TRANSPORT, transport to the next world, i.e. execute
TRAVELLER, travailer, labourer
TRICK, (i) trifle (III i 115); (ii) fashion (III ii 48, V i 502)

TROT, contemptuous term for a midwife or old woman

TROTH, BY MY TROTH, truly

TRUNCHEON, staff used as a symbol of military command

TUB, 'in the tub', (i) in the beef-salting tub; (ii) in the sweating-tub as a treatment for venereal disease (pun, III ii 52–3)

TUN-DISH, funnel (with sexual suggestion)

TURN, 'a good turn', (i) a favour; (ii) an execution (a 'turn' was the removal of the ladder from under the feet of the condemned man) (pun, IV ii 54)

TWAIN, two

UNDISCERNIBLE, impenetrably deceptive

UNFOLD, explain, reveal

UNFOLDING STAR, morning star (indicating that it is time to release the sheep from the fold)

UNGENITUR'D, sexless, without genitals

UNGOT, unbegotten

UNHURTFUL, harmless

UNKINDNESS, unnatural behaviour

UNLIKE, unlikely

UNMEET, unsuitable

UNPITIED, pitiless, merciless

UNPREGNANT, unready, unprepared

UNQUESTION'D, unconsidered, uninvestigated

UNSHAPES, upsets, disturbs

UNSHUNN'D, unshunnable, unavoidable

UNSISTING, unassisting, i.e. unopening

UNSKILFULLY, ignorantly

UNTAUGHT, unmannerly

UNTRUSSING, untying the laces which hold his hose up, i.e. undressing

UNWEDGEABLE, unsplittable

UNWEIGHING, thoughtless, undiscriminating

UNWONTED, unaccustomed, unusual

UPRIGHTEOUSLY, righteously

USE (n.), customary practice (III ii 118); 'Both thanks and use', both thanks for the loan and interest on it; 'use and liberty', habitual licence; (v.), (i) make a practice of (II i 42, IV ii 112); (ii) frequent (III ii 205)

USURIES, 'two usuries', i.e. prostitution ('the merriest') and money-lending ('the worser')

VAIL YOUR REGARD, lower your glance

VAIN, silly, foolish; 'for vain', for vanity (with pun on 'vane', weathervane)

VANITY, foolishness, conceit

VANTAGE, (i) advantage (II ii 74); (ii) advantageous position for intercepting (IV vi 11); (iii) special treatment due to high rank (V i 411)

VARLET, rascal

VASSAL, subject

VASTIDITY, vastness

VEIN, proper manner of speaking

VIEWLESS, invisible

VISITATION, 'lent him visitation', visited him

VOTARISTS OF ST CLARE, an order of nuns

VOUCH (n.), testimony; (v.), testify

VULGARLY, publicly

WAIT UPON, accompany, follow

WANT, need

WARD, (i) section of the city (II i 252); (ii) prison cell (IV iii 58, V i 10)

WARP, deviate

WARRANT (v.), guarantee, promise; 'upon a warranted need', if there is really a need for it

WARRANTS (n.), signs, appearances

WARY, careful

WEAR, fashion

WEARY, tedious, long-winded

WEIGHT, 'by weight The words of heaven', fully, according to scripture (probably Romans ix, 15–18)

WELL COME, welcome

WELL-WARRANTED, (i) given ample power and authority; (ii) thoroughly justified in a course of action

WELL-WISH'D, popular

WEND, go

WIDOW, settle a dead husband's estate upon

WILL, desire, lust (II iv 164, 175)

WIT, intelligence, good sense

WITHAL, (i) with (IV iii 138, V i 342); (ii) with them (V i 422)

WOODMAN, hunter, i.e. woman-chaser

WORM, snake

WORTH, 'worth is able', either (i) worthiness is capable; or (ii) authority is suitable (there are probably one or more lines missing between I i 9 and 10); 'her worth worth yours', see that your worth is equal to hers

WOT, know

WROUGHT BY, worked according to

YARE, ready

ZODIACS, rounds of the zodiac, i.e. years